NEAR DEA

CONQUERS
ALS, BLINDNESS, DEPRESSION, GRIEF, SUICIDE & MORE

——A Book of Hope——

"I've Had Many Miracles! And YOU Can Too!"

An Amazing True Story by
Dr. Joyce Hunt Brown

ISBN: 978-1-6382-1220-1

Library of Congress Control Number: 2021904307

Disclaimer: The content of this book is based on the author's own personal experiences and is for informational purposes only and is not intended to diagnose, treat, cure, or prevent any condition or disease, nor is it to replace the advice or care of professional health-care practitioners.

V214

Is there Hope for My Problems?

Is there a Purpose for Living?

WHAT PEOPLE ARE SAYING

"Dr. Joyce...is saving lives" and having "a life-changing impact..."

—**Mark Victor Hansen**, Author *Chicken Soup for the Soul*

"Dr. Joyce Hunt Brown is one of the most remarkable and inspiring people I have ever met. Her book *God's Heavenly Answers* has saved hundreds of people's lives who had been suicidal. After reading her book describing her near-death experience, we were so deeply touched that we made contact with her, and have been the best of friends ever since. Joyce has helped countless people deal with grief and major stress issues in their lives. It is interesting, that more recently others have shown how almost all disease, which includes suicidal tendencies, are linked to stress. Society owes a great debt of gratitude to Dr. Brown for her pioneering work and continued contributions. How fortunate we are to have her book. It, undoubtedly, will be used countless times in helping people move through their challenges in life."

—**Dr. David W. Allan**, Atomic Clock Scientist, author of *It's About Time: Science Harmonizing with Religion.* Dr. Allan is a world-renowned atomic clock physicist who helped develop the nation's atomic clock during his 32 years at NBS/NIST. He also spent many years helping in the development of GPS.

"Dr. Joyce Brown is one of the most upbeat and inspiring people we know. If you look at her life story, you will wonder how she could possibly be so upbeat. She has endured more heartbreak and trials than anyone we know. And yet, her belief in God is strong, her commitment to help her fellowman never wavers, and her positive attitude never quits. I, Kim, was diagnosed with ALS in 2011 and we relate well to that portion of her story. Many of my symptoms were the same as Dr. Brown's. In 2016, I was termed an ALS reversal. Though I have not completely healed, we continue to enjoy life and move  forward. This new book is valuable for anyone looking to improve their life in multiple ways and is totally inspiring. We hope you will read it."

—**Kim and Kay Cherry**, Founders of ALS Winners

"I have firsthand knowledge that the book *God's Heavenly Answers* is actually saving lives. The author, Dr. Joyce Brown, shatters the myth that all you have to do is kill yourself to get a heavenly place of peace and beauty. Joyce's near-death experience of being on the Other Side convinced her that every day in this life is precious, that we can't win the prize if we take a shortcut and never finish the race, and that there is purpose to every life. Joyce was suicidal from the age of eight, and when her father committed  suicide, she very nearly joined him. She often saw suicide as an option to escape the problems of this life, and consequently, often avoided the problem-solving process. Her experience on the Other Side changed her life forever. Her book should be read by every person who struggles with suicidal thoughts. To those in a position to make a difference, I hope you will lend your influence and help correct some of the false ideas that are rampant in our country. Joyce's files are steadily filling with letters from people whose lives have been saved by reading her book."

—**Darla Isackson**, *Finding Hope While Grieving Suicide*

"I have personally known Dr. Joyce Brown for many years and know her very well in all aspects of her life. I have known about her battles with pain, paralysis, Rheumatoid Arthritis, ALS, blindness, great financial losses, and the loss of loved ones. I know that it has helped her to learn patience, tolerance and the real value of health, relationships, and life. As she struggled with Agoraphobia, despair, stress, and betrayals, I believe this is why she is better able to feel compassion, empathy and a love for mankind. From my own personal experience, I know she understands better, firsthand, what so many others are going through. I have been a holistic health practitioner for over 30 years. I have learned from Joyce's near-death experience about God's special messages to prepare for my own Other Side's life review. Over all these years that I have known her, I have taken the opportunity to share with many people these eternal truths that she has taught. I have seen results people have had after Dr. Joyce conducted seminars, speaking engagements, coaching, and sharing her unique coping techniques, including anger management, and helping them overcome depression. She has guided people to take responsibilities for their lives and future, rather than blaming someone else for their problems and past mistakes, as they also found their own purpose for living. Dr. Joyce has had many productive counseling sessions with people of all ages, including working with the youth, and especially in detention centers and prisons in Utah and California where she shared her Other Side experience to sizable, captured, audiences. I'm still learning things from her many experiences and I consider her an eternal friend and believe we will know each other forever."

—**N. Louise Ferguson**, a close friend & colleague of Dr. Joyce

DEDICATION

This book is dedicated to sharing God's message with the world. God is real. He is filled with love. And He is by your side throughout your life's journey.

Our mission is to change and save lives. Through our books, audiobooks, and other information products, we share proven, practical knowledge and timeless wisdom with people who need to overcome stress, grief, depression, health ailments, suicide, and more.

This is a book of hope, created to help each person find their own purpose for living. All proceeds from this book are donated to this cause.

Stress and Grief Relief, Inc., 501(c)(3) is a life-changing and lifesaving non-profit organization. All donations are tax deductible (EIN: 95-472-2033).

Stress and Grief Relief, Inc.
450 Hillside Drive # A 224,
Mesquite, NV 89027.

1-800-734-3439
www.HopeDr.org

ABBREVIATIONS

The following are some of the frequently used abbreviations found in this book:

ALS: Amyotrophic Lateral Sclerosis, also known as Lou Gehrig's Disease.
IANDS: International Association for Near Death Studies.
NDE: Near Death Experience.
NSA: National Speakers Association.
PMA: Positive Mental Attitude.

TABLE OF CONTENTS

CHAPTER 1

MIRACLES DO HAPPEN

In 1988, at 54 years old, Joyce Brown was diagnosed with ALS, in addition to myasthenia gravis. She was a busy professional, a business owner, and the mother of three grown children. Her neurologist estimated she had five months to live, but Joyce knew miracles were possible. Today, at almost 90 years old, she has overcome a number of serious life challenges, including ALS.

We met Joyce in 2014 while filming ALS reversals, an incredibly special group of people who have overcome this terminal disease. Joyce's unwavering positive attitude in the face of seemingly insurmountable challenges, her quick mind well into her late 80's and her ability to find joy and purpose in life no matter what, are just three of the reasons she succeeded in beating ALS. We hope you enjoy Dr. Joyce Brown's wisdom and healing journey as much as we did.

—Patricia Tamowski & Scott Douglas,
www.HealingALS.org

CHAPTER 2

WHY I WROTE THIS BOOK: TO GIVE YOU HOPE—DEATH IS NOT THE END, THERE IS LIFE AFTER LIFE

After pleading with God to die, and then getting a glimpse of Heaven and Hell, I knew I had to write this book. Death is *not* the end. There *is* life after life.

My life has been filled with challenges and calamities, but also many miracles. This is the story of my life before and after I died in 1983, and was given another chance to live with a new purpose. It is also about my life before and after being healed of ALS in 1988. This book includes heavenly answers to earthly questions, wisdom I've gained as a result of the many challenges I've conquered, and the stories around the many miracles I've received throughout my life.

In 1983, I returned to life as a transformed person, knowing I had a definite purpose for living and, therefore, that I had to make it through challenges rather than giving up because of them—and to help others do the same.

It is my hope that the answers I received and the wisdom I learned may be used by others in their own lives so they may find hope, healing and relief from stress, depression and grief. Having lost six members of my family to suicide, and the death of other family and friends, I understand the grief that comes from losing loved ones and others you sincerely care about.

One of the most encouraging things I found when I was on the Other Side is that we *will* see our loved ones again. If we could just hear the message they are trying to tell us, we would know how much they care, and how much they want us to use our remaining time wisely.

Since COVID-19 has raged around the world, there has been a huge increase in depression, anxiety, and grief, both from the loss of friends and loved ones, but also from the extreme changes the virus has forced us to endure. All of this has led to

2

an unprecedented rise in suicides.

Regardless of the problems we are facing, there are no easy solutions. The answers are the same as those I found for the multiple problems, challenges and calamities I faced during my life. The only way we can improve our situations is by getting control of our thoughts, feelings, and actions, with courage, faith, hope, and a *definite chief purpose for living.* We need to endure as best we can, one hour at a time if need be. As we seek relief from stress and grief, call upon the powers of Heaven, and help and serve others, we may reap miracles.

This book is written from my heart to yours.

Truly, with Divine intervention, I have cheated death numerous times, including surviving car accidents, overcoming major illnesses, living through other life-threatening disastrous events, as well as actually dying and returning to my body.

Over the years, there have been millions of reported near-death experiences (NDE). These profound, transformational life experiences are becoming more well-known to the general public.

It's surprising how many people I have personally met after sharing my story of dying and going to the Other Side who told me they too had a near-death experience. There are commonalties, yet each experience is unique and different in their own ways.

Thousands of books have been written about people's

experiences, including several by Arvin Gibson and David Bennett. Arvin Gibson was a good friend and mentor. He greatly encouraged me to get my book, *God's Heavenly Answers*, written and published. Afterward, he told me he felt that my book contained special NDE information that people would want to know and read about for years after we are both gone.

He was also instrumental in helping the world become more aware of the many near-death experiences that were being reported. Although Arvin didn't have a near-death experience himself, he was fascinated by the phenomenon. Before he wrote each of his books, he would interview dozens of people who had a near-death experience. He would choose the most interesting stories, and then verify their information before including them in his books.

He found during their experience they had many things in common, which he then documented them. Some describe going through a tunnel, others are just up and out of their bodies as I was. They all realized they were in a different realm. Most meet a bright, white light and they have an overwhelming knowledge that God is real. Earth life is not the true world. Most people who have an NDE have a panoramic life review, which gives them a new perspective of their own life on Earth, and reasons to make it through challenges.

Some wanted to stay on the Other Side, but were told they had to go back. They had not finished their purpose for living, which could affect generations to come. Others wanted to return to Earth life because they felt they were needed by family and friends.

One of the telltale signs of someone having a near-death experience is when they come back a transformed person, with a driving purpose for living and a desire to share it with all who will listen.

When interviewing people, Arvin discovered almost all of the near-death survivors had the same belief as to who God is, just as they did before they had their NDE.

The case of Howard Storm is an interesting exception. Storm wrote a book about his experience titled: *My Descent into Death*. He died a confirmed atheist. He descended into what he described as Hell after his death. He then called upon Jesus Christ to save him. He came back to life a confirmed Christian and became pastor of a church.

The International Association for Near-Death Studies (IANDS) has group leaders and chapters all over the world where people can go and tell about their unique NDE, and where those interested can go to listen. I am the IANDS group leader for the chapters in St. George, Utah as well as Las Vegas and Mesquite, Nevada.

David Bennett, the IANDS Groups Coordinator and Board Member at Large also had a fascinating, in-depth near-death experience, as you will read in a later chapter (don't miss his story!). With the knowledge and determination he gained from having been on the Other Side, he was able to completely heal himself within six months of the time he was diagnosed with stage IV lung cancer. David has written several books, including *Voyage of Purpose*, and remains very active with the IANDS organization.

Having a near-death experience is a great life changing miracle. We all have many more miracles than we realize. Not until we are on the Other Side, and are able to see each of our own lives from an eternal perspective, will we be able to know just how many miracles we have each had.

I have had many miracles and you can too. As I share some of my miraculous experiences, perhaps it will inspire you with additional hope and faith to receive miracles as well. I know of countless others who have received miracles, a number of which you will learn more about toward the end of this book (see Conquering Heroes section), and, through my non-profit work, I continue to meet new people and hear new stories of still others who have received miracles.

Usually, in order to receive miracles, we have to do all that we can. This includes a number of things I have learned and will share with you in this book, including unique coping techniques for life's various challenges, as well as for stress, grief relief, depression, and even suicide prevention. Miracles, I have found, are preceded by a number of things, including positive beliefs and actions, but even more importantly, having courage, faith and really trusting in and listening to God. Utilizing this information can also help you gain eternal peace of mind.

CHAPTER 3

MY CHILDHOOD

This is where my story begins.

From the time I was a small child, I felt unloved, unwanted and that I was a big burden for having been born. I was born in the fall of 1933 during the Great Depression. My father did not want me because I was not a boy.

When I was about eighteen months old, he dropped my mother and me off at her parents' farm. He left us there with no means of support, and he never came back.

My parents divorced soon after.

I remember seeing my father perhaps three or four times during my childhood.

As soon as she was able, my mother moved us to Pocatello, Idaho. It was still during the Great Depression. Many banks and businesses were closed, jobs were scarce, and millions struggled just to get food. Mother found a job scrubbing floors at a hotel.

She told me that there were many times she had to leave me crying in a bathtub, but she had no choice. She was so busy as a struggling single mom, trying to make a living and take care of us.

She was often sad, and cried a lot. When I was three or four years old, I remember sitting in a little rocking chair just wanting to be good and not cause problems that would make Mother feel worse.

In addition, I had bad cases of whooping cough, mumps and measles, and the whole time feared I might make my mother cry. Chicken pox at least waited until I was much older.

Being an only child, without other family for guidance or direction, I felt confused, lonely and unhappy. At times, I just wanted to disappear. But, I didn't realize how hard this situation was on my mother, too.

When I was not quite six years old, I started school in first grade. I knew I didn't fit in. The other kids didn't like me. They made fun of my clothes. When I walked, they could see my shoes had cardboard in them to cover the holes in the bottoms. After only about two weeks of school, I told the teacher I was quitting and not coming back any more. I told her I had learned to sign my name, count my money, and I didn't need to learn anything else.

I did not know where I was going to get the money I would be counting, but I thoroughly believed that was all I needed to know.

The next thing I knew, they had contacted my mother to come in and talk to the principal. I remember sitting on a bench outside the office while they were talking. I felt this was a useless meeting. I had made up my mind. I was not going to school any more. When they came out of their meeting, they informed me I was going back to school for many years to come. When I heard their decision, it made me cry. Unhappily, I realized they could force me to go to school, but my mind and heart would not be there.

It was many years of wasted time in my life before I discovered the value of learning and education. With my mother so busy having to work and with her own problems, I felt like an orphan and a big burden to her throughout my life.

When I was six and a half years old, a family friend seriously molested me. This just added to my confusion and unhappiness. My mother did not believe me, which created more hurt. With all the difficulties she was going through, I don't think she realized how serious it was.

When I was in second grade, 7 years old, one day at school, the teacher came down to my desk and asked me a question about our lesson that day. I had not fully understood the question. When I didn't give the answer she wanted, she got angry and suddenly struck me with her cupped hand on the left side of my head, right over my ear. Immediately, I heard a loud ringing and lost a large part of my hearing. This caused permanent damage. The situation was basically ignored.

However, by the sixth grade, the principal and teachers decided I needed to take lip-reading classes which I did for the next four years. They greatly helped compensate for my hearing loss.

When I was eight years old, my mother took me with her to a funeral. They talked about how happy the person was who died and how nice it is in Heaven. They spoke as if they KNEW this for certain, as if they had all been there before.

It sounded wonderful. About a month later, I learned about suicide and decided that it was what I wanted to do, believing I could just go and be happy in Heaven. I am a very practical person. Why stay in this world with all of its problems, if I could just die and go to Heaven and be happy?

From this point on, giving up and thinking of going to Heaven became a way of life.

Joyce with her army helmet as protection from bullies with rocks.

When I was about ten years old some information surfaced and Mother told me she now believed I had been molested. I knew she was deeply sorry about it. She hadn't realized how bad it was and how much it affected me, but with all that was going on in her life at the time, she did not know what to do about it. I was glad she at least acknowledged it.

However, I had mentally moved on and by this time I had new problems. As an overweight and combative child, I was bullied and was the brunt of schoolyard jokes.

Being overweight, I was taunted and teased. Kids even threw rocks at me. I found an army helmet to protect my head during these rock fights.

One morning, also at age ten, I woke up with severe pain in my side and was sick to my stomach. Mother took me to the doctor, who admitted me to the hospital. They had no time to tell me what was happening, and I was naturally afraid.

As I was on a gurney being wheeled down to the operating room, a nurse looked down at me and said in a loud voice, "She is so fat. She's huge." For a 10-year old not knowing what was happening, that was devastating.

Tears began to roll down my face, and by the time we got to the operating room, I was sobbing with fright and embarrassment.

People need to realize that words can hit as hard as a fist.

I found out after my surgery that my appendix was about to burst. This was one of my first of many miracles.

CHAPTER 4

TROUBLED TEENS AND MORE MIRACLES

At age 12, I had a case of rheumatic fever that was so severe it was a miracle I survived. For a few years afterwards, it left me with weaknesses and complications. I was no longer able to ride a bike, climb stairs, or take physical education in school. However, miraculously, during my teen years, I recovered my strength, and did not have any long-term complications.

As I grew into a young woman, I became shy, anxious, fearful, and reclusive. When I was about 15, I came down with a severe case of chicken pox that lasted over three weeks, which added to my feelings of loneliness and depression.

I did not understand why God would not let me die. I had prayed and prayed that He would please take me to Heaven. Suicide was always in the back of my mind.

Within a few months, I turned 16 and my mother had remarried. I felt even more out of place.

I called and made arrangements to go live with my father in Idaho, even though I hadn't seen him in years. He had remarried and I had a half-brother and a half-sister who were about four and five years old.

Things went well for the first few days. I enjoyed visiting with some cousins I hadn't met before. I thought this was a dream come true. It felt like I finally was part of a family.

One day while visiting with a cousin, we had a big argument. I don't remember what it was about, but seemed very important at the time. I went back to the house where I was living with my dad, the family had just sat down to eat dinner.

When I came in, I told my dad about the argument with my cousin. He jumped up, grabbed hold of my clothes, threw me over into a corner of the room, and made me stand with my face to the wall. He said, I should have been able to solve all my own problems. I was not to come home a loser.

I stood in the corner, went without dinner and felt devastated, crushed and embarrassed, sobbing as they started eating. Dreams of having a life with my father had just crashed down around me. After the meal was over, I was permitted to go to bed with no dinner.

The next day, my dad told me he had a car he needed me to drive. He explained that it wasn't registered and, to avoid being ticketed, he wanted me to follow him through the back roads, which meant going up a mountain on a single lane dirt road.

Even though I was frightened, and didn't want to drive the car, I didn't dare tell him no. It was winter and the roads were icy. Also, I had just barely gotten my driver's license, and had never driven on ice or snow.

As I followed him on back roads, we finally came to a rather steep mountain road. Almost at the top of the hill, the car began to slide backwards on the ice. Within seconds, the car was careening toward the edge of the road. Inches from the edge, with no guardrail, was a two or three hundred foot drop off. I could barely see the bottom over the side.

No matter what I tried to do, no matter how much or how little I pressed the gas pedal, the car just continued to slide toward the edge. The brakes wouldn't hold either. The car just kept sliding. I gripped the steering wheel tightly, closing my eyes and waiting for the fall to come.

Suddenly, out of nowhere, I felt a big bang on the back of the car. I looked in the rearview mirror, and saw a huge Idaho Power truck. It seemed to come out of nowhere.

The driver began pushing my car back up on the road and over the top of the hill. I couldn't believe it! I was saved!

Once I knew for sure that I was safe and free of the ice, I was going to pull over to thank the driver for saving my life. But when I looked up into the rearview mirror, the truck was gone. It just vanished. I kept thinking how there were no side streets, and how it was impossible that he could have turned around on such a narrow road. I soon decided it must have been a life-saving gift from God.

I didn't realize it at the time, but this was one of my life's many miracles. Apparently, I had not yet fulfilled my life's purpose.

Within the next few days, I begged my mother, who finally agreed to let me come back home to live with her.

During my teen years I did lose weight, to the point that I developed an eating disorder, and became anorexic.

CHAPTER 5

FATHER'S NEAR-DEATH EXPERIENCE

At age 17, my father was traveling through a city nearby and was in a serious car accident. I went to visit him in the hospital.

He told me that during the accident he left his body and looked down, watching as the medics were working on him.

He also told me beauty and peace surrounded him, and he did not want to come back to life. This only reinforced my belief about Heaven, and my wish to die and go there.

At that time, I did not know that this beauty and peace he described is for people who have earned it during their limited Earth life, and who die in God's timing, not their own.

CHAPTER 6

FROM THE FRYING PAN TO THE FIRE

For my 18th birthday, using money I had earned from helping a neighbor clean her house, I went to a diner, sat on a stool at the counter, and ordered cake and ice cream to celebrate. While I was sitting there, a handsome cab driver sat next to me. He ordered coffee and lit his cigarette.

A few puffs later, he started up a conversation. His words were very charming, and he had big blue eyes like my father's. I soon agreed to a date even though he was 11 years older than I was. After the date and more charming words, I fell head over heels in love.

When he proposed, this seemed like the perfect way to escape my unhappy home life. Two and a half weeks after our first meeting, we were married. However, right away I realized that my Prince Charming and I had nothing in common and were sorrowfully incompatible.

In addition, I now had a 7-year-old stepson named Doyle from my husband's previous marriage. He was a sweet little boy, but, having just turned eighteen, I didn't have much experience even being around small children. I had no idea how to be a mother, let alone a step-mother—especially with all the other challenges we had in our marriage.

I had just jumped out of the frying pan, and into the fire.

Moving back home with my mother was not an option. I had to figure out how I could get out of this regrettable marriage. I felt desperately trapped.

Not knowing what else to do, I frantically called the clergy and asked him if there was any way he could not file that marriage certificate. I did not realize the legal entanglements to get out of an ill-fated marriage.

One of the very most important decisions a person can make is choosing a proper mate to spend their life with. What will their family life be like together? Will it be loving and fulfilling or filled with regrets, heartaches, and abuse?

CHAPTER 7

IF ONLY

At 19, I was pregnant. In addition to caring for my step-son, to earn money for the family, I tended an additional three children day and night, whose mothers had health problems. Their ages were about four to eight years old. On top of all this I had the many challenges of being pregnant, including morning-sickness.

I took care of them 24 hours a day for several months. Unfortunately, all four children came down with chicken pox at about the same time. At least there was the miracle that I had already had chicken pox.

I hated life and I continually prayed to God that I would die. At 19 years old, I felt my life was hopeless.

As if this were not enough stress, my husband's brother and one of his friends also moved in with us.

I was cooking, baking homemade bread, and cleaning for all of us on top of being pregnant.

I vividly remember feeling extremely overwhelmed and depressed. There was no way for me to get out of this situation. I was trapped. Repeatedly, I pleaded with God to let me die. I harbored the false belief that my

Joyce with family laundry at age 19.

death was the only answer to all my problems.

My thoughts were full of "if only."

If only I had not gotten married so young without really knowing the man with whom I was to spend my life.

If only I had chosen a compatible husband with mutual interests and goals.

If only I had a better education so I could support my expected new baby and myself.

If only I could disappear and DIE.

I prayed and prayed to God to become a new person. If I was not going to die, please just help me to change.

Now as I share my experience with the youth, I plead with them to learn from my mistakes.

CHAPTER 8

A LIFE CHANGING MIRACLE

Finally, after several years, thinking over my miserable life to this point, and wanting to become a completely different person, a new miracle came into my life.

Praying and praying, I soon discovered unique *sleep learning* courses that, as I listened to them, changed my negative thinking to positive feelings and actions.

I desperately, and with *consistent* determination, listened to them day and night.

I gained new confidence and direction as the constant repetitions of positive affirmations reprogrammed my negative thinking.

It worked dramatic wonders in my life, and I had new confidence and self-esteem. For a brief time, I even did some modeling on TV, and in the newspaper.

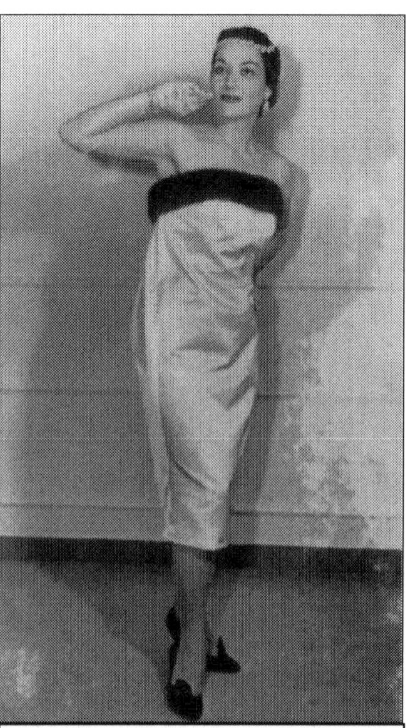

Joyce modeling after her changes from sleep learning.

After I learned I was expected to attend a party as an escort to one of the executives, I turned down a lucrative contract for a cigarette company. After one too many of these sort of requests, I soon realized there was no future for me in modeling.

CHAPTER 9

LIFE AS A SINGLE MOM

Unfortunately, I had married young, like my mother, and was terrified of becoming a single mom as she had been.

After about eight years in this heartbreaking marriage, I had three wonderful children, two daughters and a son. However, the situation was too overwhelming. Finally, in the fall of 1959, at the age of 26, I managed to get a divorce.

I found out the hard way, by not choosing to marry the right, compatible companion, usually separation and a bitter divorce will follow. Divorce can cause a loss of happy, family times together, disrupted and lonely holiday seasons, and the loss of close family ties from then on. This loss of family closeness may even include being almost totally alone for end-of-life care.

Most divorces can leave traumatic effects on the family.

CHAPTER 10

THE POWER OF SLEEP LEARNING: HOW CAN WE LEARN WHILE WE SLEEP?

Every night when we go to sleep, our conscious mind goes to sleep. Our subconscious mind, however, is awake and able to accept positive affirmations. This changes our thoughts and feelings, and helps create our ideal self, with potential for miraculous results. It did this for me, and countless others. It can do it for you, too.

By using an effective *sleep learning* system, with powerful positive affirmations, you can unconsciously change your self-talk which can change your life, helping you become your ideal self.

How often have you heard the expression, "Let me sleep on it"? Whether people realize it or not, our unconscious minds are continuously working to help us make decisions and solve problems, even while we sleep. What most people do not realize is that you can work more effectively with your unconscious mind to better tap your brain's miraculous power.

Joyce modeling on television.

In fact, with *sleep learning,* you can implant into your unconscious mind proper suggestions and thought patterns of courage, confidence, and right thinking, feelings, and actions which later benefit your everyday, conscious living. *Desire, visualize* and, with the help of God, you can *realize* miraculous results in your life.

As I continued to listen to the *sleep learning* courses, I began to replace my negative thinking with positive beliefs while I slept or meditated. They helped me to move forward with new confidence and determination.

I became a new, vibrant person. My memory increased to where I had an almost photographic memory. A test confirmed my ability to speed read at over 950 words per minute with almost perfect comprehension.

I studied real estate for a short time, and I passed the exam easily. I became a licensed real estate agent, and sold some properties. The future looked promising.

I was beginning to understand the remarkable power of the human mind. It really is astonishing what you can do when your mind is working for you instead of against you.

CHAPTER 11

TRAGIC AUTO ACCIDENT AND AFTER-EFFECTS

In July of 1960, at the age of 27, because of a careless driver, I was seriously injured in a terrible car accident. Even though I had a lot of severe pain from the whiplash, and a serious injury to my lower back, I had to endure it for a year and a half before the driver's insurance would pay for the cervical neck and lower back surgery. By not having a very good attorney, I was disappointed that the money barely covered the attorney's costs, the doctors and the hospital. Also, I had lost precious time with my children while I recovered.

During such complicated surgeries and recoveries my children had to be cared for by others. I simply was not physically able to care for them myself.

When they operated, they found there were two herniated disks which required bone fusions. They surgically obtained the donor bone from my hip to fuse into my neck. Recovery from the hip surgery was more painful and complicated and greatly delayed my recovery and made it difficult to even get in and out of bed.

About two months later, I thought I was making great progress after the surgery. I drove to the store for some essential items. While I was stopped for a red light, the unimaginable happened. Unexpectedly, a car crashed into the back of mine. My neck snapped backwards causing another whiplash and broke loose the two previous fusions.

This ultimately required another two cervical neck fusions, and another donor bone surgery from my other hip. This involved additional recovery time and prolonged incapacitation. From my previous experience, and to avoid disheartening attorneys, court involvement and delays, I accepted their discouragingly low offer of only $6,000 and arranged for the payments to go directly to the doctors and hospital.

This additional surgery resulted in more time delays, and

required a longer recovery with both hips painfully disabled.

I was overwhelmed as a single mom in this fragile condition caring for my children, Suzan, Patty, and David. They had multiple trips to the emergency room with life threatening bouts of croup, strep-throat, and severe tonsillitis, plus having to have tonsillectomies.

After their tonsillectomies I had to arrange for them to be cared for by others while I had my own surgeries. I was very depressed, worried about the future, and missed my children terribly while going through this nightmare situation. My heart ached not being able to be with them. I missed some of the most precious moments of their childhood. In my other book, *God's Heavenly Answers*, I go into more details about the anguishing trials and heartbreak of these situations with my children.

Recently, when I was going through some old files, I found a poem I wrote expressing how I felt at the time:

MY PRAYER

Oh, my Father in Heaven above.
       Show me Thy mercy and Thy love.
Things have happened here in my life.
       Which have caused me much grief and strife.

My strength is gone. My spirit is weak.
       And of your power and help I seek.
My mortal eyes just cannot see,
       Any way that is left open to me.

To solve these problems that are so great
       That will control my future and my fate
Must I be so terribly distraught,
       Without thy guidance my hope is naught.

Three little spirits you've given to me
       To guide and direct till they return to Thee.
Their cries ring loudly in my ears,
       But I'm too far away to soothe their fears.

Oh God, be with them and comfort their souls
       That the spirits of evil won't take their tolls.
Help us to conquer this illness and pain
       The cause of the separation of which I disdain.

Help us to meet these greatly mounting debts
       Which have added so much to our sorrows and frets.
How I ache for my three babies so fair.
       To hold them close so they know I still care.

Father bless us with health and strength,
       That we may enjoy life to a good length.
Grant us the ability, determination and drive
       To live more Christ-like as long as we're alive.

God, I'd humbly ask and I pray,
       If it can be Thy will, that maybe today
An answer might come.
                   Joyce Hunt (1962)

I had to have eight major spinal surgeries over the next fifteen years that ended up being very traumatic and unsuccessful. Four of them were bone fusions in the neck and cervical area, and four were in the lower spine.

As a result, I was almost constantly in tremendous pain. My circumstances during this time were indescribably difficult to bear, including extreme spinal and balance problems that continue to this day.

After the tragic auto accident, and between surgeries, there were family situations that seemed overwhelming. There were some good times where it seemed my life was going to be much better. But then there were sudden, unexpected down turns between surgeries where it seemed impossible for me to endure.

However, every time I went to the hospital for surgery, I took my special record player and *sleep learning* recordings, which helped with relaxation, pain relief and to prevent depression because of my situation. It was so important for me to keep up with the positive thinking and hope for a better future. I wanted to receive mental miracles.

With all the positive thinking, *sleep learning* didn't change my life-time beliefs in the myth that all I had to do was die in order to receive an unearned peace.

Frustration, despair, and despondency took over because of the pain of so many surgeries. All of this led me to feelings of hopelessness, deep depression, and two failed suicide attempts. I just wanted to die.

At that time, I did not know that sometimes we can get so wrapped up in the present that we do not realize the future can hold wondrous changes.

CHAPTER 12

KEEP ON KEEPING ON

There were short periods of time when it seemed like I was going to have some happiness and joy, only to have tragic life events crash down on me with compounding sorrows and heartaches that reinforced my belief that suicide was the only answer.

Throughout this period, I continued listening to the *sleep learning* recordings to create miracles and to get out of this situation and live a better life. I felt trapped and needed to gain control of my thinking no matter the pain or how many problems I had. I always felt more relaxed and less stressed as I listened to positive affirmations, such as: "I am calm, I am serene, I am confident, I enjoy life. I feel health and well-being all through my mind and my body."

I thought about the story I'd heard of two frogs in a bucket of cream.

They could not get out. One of them gave up, fell to the bottom, and drowned.

The other was determined to keep swimming. As he paddled and paddled, he turned the cream to butter, and was able to jump out.

CHAPTER 13

BOTCHED SPINAL SURGERY

In the spring of 1973 at age 39, a lumbar, lower back surgery by a surgeon I will refer to as "Dr. B," dramatically changed my life forever.

This horrifically botched surgery caused continuous excruciating pain and dropped foot.

After I was released from the hospital, I was required to wear a leg and foot brace in order to walk at all. This surgery was so outlandish and bizarre that it was suspected the surgeon was using illegal drugs.

Sometimes the more things seem hopeless, the bigger the miracle is needed, but we just have to "keep on keeping on."

CHAPTER 14

ANOTHER DEVELOPMENT

For the last several years I had been consulting my gynecologist regarding additional health difficulties. He told me he believed my symptoms could have been cancerous.

I finally agreed to set aside some time in January 1974 to go to the hospital for exploratory surgery. He did find giant cysts that needed to be surgically removed, but none were cancerous. Even though it was good news, it required additional weeks of limited activity while I was recovering.

CHAPTER 15

AFTER EFFECTS OF THE BOTCHED SPINAL SURGERY

Toward the first of June, 1974, at the age of 40, after desperately searching, I finally found an orthopedic surgeon who agreed to try to help reverse the extensive injuries caused by "Dr. B."

The damage to my spinal cord and the paralysis was so serious he did not know if he could help me.

The surgery took several hours and was partially successful for relieving some of the pain and paralysis. However, it was such a small amount that I could hardly tell the difference.

Right after the surgery, while I was still waking from the anesthetic in the recovery room, the surgeon came in to see me. Somehow, I knew, and I told him emphatically, that he had not gotten all of the sutures off which were wrapped around my spinal cord.

He answered me, "You can't know that. And we did get them all."

After about a year of extreme pain, and pleading with the Doctors to do a special test, that would determine whether there was still pressure on the spinal cord, they finally agreed, just to pacify me, and did it.

They were shocked to find out that what I was saying was true. It showed on the fluoroscope and the X-rays they had not gotten all the sutures off and there was still significant pressure on my spinal cord.

After the tests, one of the doctors came in the room and told me that for legal reasons they would all have to resign, and could not talk to me about my case any further. It would be up to me to find a different orthopedic surgeon for additional treatments for my spinal condition.

I was still left with extreme pain and lost most of the use of my left leg and foot. I felt dismay, despair, and wondered what I could do. A short time later, I managed to get a copy of my X-rays and took them to the neurology department at a leading university hospital.

CHAPTER 16

PRAYERS FOR LIFE OR DEATH

For the next several months, I was left in this painful, debilitating condition. Being a very active person, this greatly slowed me down, but did not stop me.

By this time, my mom and three-year old granddaughter, Crystal, came to live with me. I was glad to have their company. Continuing to search for another surgeon, I went to the neurology department at a top university with my x-rays. Along the way, I stopped at a photography shop and had black and white copies made of the x-rays, which I still have today.

After their neurology team examined me and studied the x-rays, their top neurologist said words no one ever wants to hear. Tears welled up, and my heart almost stopped as I heard them say, "Your condition is hopeless and nothing more can be done." I simply needed to accept the fact that I was disabled and would just have to live with the paralysis and pain for the rest of my life.

Driving home, I was baffled and devastated. I could not believe what I had just been told. Arriving home, my mother was anxious to hear what the doctors had to say. She was expecting good news, that they could help me. She and I both cried, wondering what the future would hold. What in the world was I going to do?

I could not accept the doctors' pronouncement, or their finality of my condition and future. At that time, I felt I had to find a better answer or die. My prayers for relief or death seemed to go unheard and unanswered.

31

CHAPTER 17

POSITIVE BELIEF

My situation seemed futile. However, I continued searching for another surgeon for a year and a half.

Fortunately, there was nothing wrong with my right foot and leg and I was very capable of driving.

Finally, in late fall of 1975, at age 42, I found a top rated, highly recommended orthopedic surgeon. He agreed the surgery was needed in an effort to relieve some of the remaining damage and pressure on my spinal cord.

The extensive surgery was performed, including a massive donated bone graft fusion.

A week after this surgery, I went home. My leg and foot seemed much better. However, complications developed with my lower back area. I did not think my back pain could get any worse. But within a short time, a more painful condition of undetermined origin set in.

Unable to tolerate this new, worsening spinal condition, I called the doctor who made arrangements with the ambulance to pick me up and readmit me to the hospital.

The anticipation of being moved was almost intolerable, but as the medical technicians took me down the steps on the gurney, the unthinkable happened.

They dropped me. I nearly passed out.

After being admitted to the hospital, additional specialists were called in.

Soon, the most sophisticated tests that were available at the time were performed, but it was all to no avail.

It seemed that I would be permanently left in this agonizing state of existence with only the use of my arms, hands, mind, and voice.

The muscles in my body were atrophying at an accelerating speed. My leg muscles hung shriveled and limp from my protruding bones from not being able to move.

My doctor, a renowned orthopedic surgeon, a marvelous man whom I greatly appreciated and respected, delivered this heartrending message to me himself. The hospital's policy was that a patient could not remain in their care under hopeless conditions. I was told that my hospital room had to be vacated for someone with hope of recovery.

He had already made arrangements with a nursing home without telling me. A gurney was brought to take me by ambulance to my new residence.

Even though I was feeling shock and dismay, I asked my doctor if he believed in God.

When he replied that he did, I said, "I need more time; I will walk again. I believe in miracles."

I was still continuously listening to my *sleep learning* recordings to help reinforce my willed determination for my body to heal and walk again. I knew that with courage, faith, prayer, and positive thinking I would receive miracles.

It's amazing, the miraculous results that can be achieved by having faith, praying, and searching for answers rather than giving up. I did not accept what I was told about my condition.

Knowing how much my mom, and my now four-year old granddaughter, Crystal, needed me, I thoroughly believed I would recover and would even walk again. My mom and Crystal were a tremendous help during my surgery recovery and my heart is filled with gratitude and appreciation for both. Crystal still holds a special place in my heart.

When my mental attitude was down and depressed, I wanted to die; when it was up, as it was then, I believed in miracles. I didn't realize how much my moods and thoughts affected other family members and those around me.

I seldom read the newspapers that were brought each morning with my breakfast tray. However, this time, an article caught my attention. I showed the doctor the story about a lady who had an ankle injury for about three years and was healed in three weeks after using a TENS Unit (Transcutaneous Electrical Nerve Stimulation).

This unit helps block some of the pain and promotes healing. The doctor ordered one immediately. Within ten days, I improved enough to be released from the hospital.

With a hospital bed in the living room of my house and the help of my mom and little granddaughter, I was able to go home.

CHAPTER 18

LIVING IN A SPINNING WORLD

In early February of 1976, additional tests revealed I had an extreme infection between the discs that had not shown up in any of the previous tests. It was called an *intervertebral disc space infection*. I was prescribed the antibiotic streptomycin.

However, a side effect and my body's reaction caused acute inner ear dysfunction, which resulted in the permanent 100 percent loss of my balance (bi-labyrinthine dysfunction), which I still live with today.

CHAPTER 19

HEALING AND LEARNING

In 1976, the United States and most of the Western world was in the midst of the energy crisis. The possible effects of the ongoing energy shortages had sparked widespread concern, and even fear. I too was becoming increasingly aware of the issues, and interested in finding answers to the problems. A friend who was a CEO for a company that was working on possible solutions invited me to go out to lunch and talk about it in more detail.

In spite of my surgeries and physical handicaps, I made sure to go. I was interested in learning about and becoming more active in this area.

Along with the energy crisis and our nation's dependency on foreign oil, we discussed the critical environmental issues the world was facing at the time. What seemed most apparent to me at the time was the need for a technology to emerge that could create energy from waste materials. For some reason, the idea seemed so fascinating to me that I decided to devote myself to learning all that I could about alternative energy.

Later that year, my condition had improved greatly. The antibiotics helped the infection in my back which helped to relieve much of the pain. The remaining pain I could mask. I also learned to adapt to my spinning world, and no longer needed the leg and foot braces.

With all I was learning about the need for and possibilities of alternative energy, I found a determination to do something about it.

In the late 1970s, I found it was difficult for women to be taken seriously in business. I made sure I maintained a professional persona. I used my maiden name and started J.E. Hunt & Associates for acquiring contracts for the engineering and construction of alternative energy projects and facilities.

I was able to arrange for a loan that I used to increase my education. I traveled to conferences and seminars across the

U.S., from Chicago and Indiana to Kentucky and California, which opened the door for meetings with top scientists and engineers from around the world.

After additional intense study and hard work, in 1978, at the age of 44, my efforts had paid off. I was able to obtain marketing rights for a unique pollution-free patented process where we could convert non-recyclable waste to energy. I was also able to get my A-100 Engineering Contractor's license so I could build and own the resource energy and recovery plant.

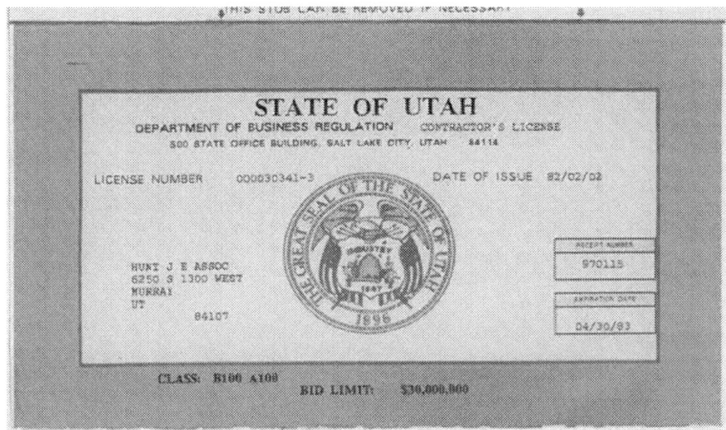

CHAPTER 20

CONVERTING GARBAGE TO ELECTRICAL ENERGY

In the spring of 1978, a large U.S. county put out a request for a proposal to take them out of the garbage business. The county was handling about 500 tons a day of solid waste. I decided that I could put all the pieces together that it would take to create a winning bid.

Although several other companies, some that were well established, presented proposals, the one I put together was unanimously accepted with a contract for 20 years.

This was a lucrative multi-million dollar recycling and waste-to-energy project. When it all came together, there were 35 employees and we processed approximately 500 tons a day of waste.

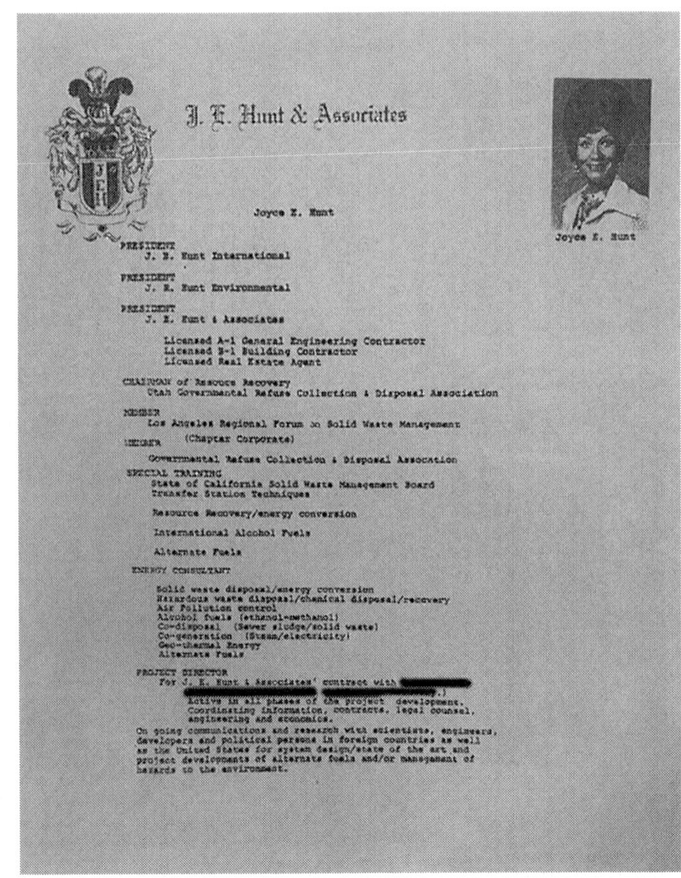

J. E. Hunt & Associates

Joyce E. Hunt

PRESIDENT
    J. E. Hunt International

PRESIDENT
    J. E. Hunt Environmental

PRESIDENT
    J. E. Hunt & Associates

        Licensed A-1 General Engineering Contractor
        Licensed B-1 Building Contractor
        Licensed Real Estate Agent

CHAIRMAN of Resource Recovery
    Utah Governmental Refuse Collection & Disposal Association

MEMBER
    Los Angeles Regional Forum on Solid Waste Management

MEMBER   (Chapter Corporate)

    Governmental Refuse Collection & Disposal Association

SPECIAL TRAINING
    State of California Solid Waste Management Board
    Transfer Station Techniques

    Resource Recovery/energy conversion

    International Alcohol Fuels

    Alternate Fuels

ENERGY CONSULTANT

    Solid waste disposal/energy conversion
    Hazardous waste disposal/chemical disposal/recovery
    Air Pollution control
    Alcohol fuels (ethanol-methanol)
    Co-disposal (Sewer sludge/solid waste)
    Co-generation (Steam/electricity)
    Geo-thermal Energy
    Alternate Fuels

PROJECT DIRECTOR
    For J. E. Hunt & Associates' contract with ▓▓▓▓▓▓
    ▓▓▓▓▓▓▓▓.)
        Active in all phases of the project development.
        Coordinating information, contracts, legal counsel,
        engineering and economics.

On going communications and research with scientists, engineers,
developers and political persons in foreign countries as well
as the United States for system design/state of the art and
project developments of alternate fuels and/or management of
hazards to the environment.

In this process, two pounds of garbage was equivalent to one pound of coal in BTU value. Our 500 tons of waste per day would produce enough electricity to light about 5,000 homes.

This was cutting-edge technology and over the next few years, top engineers came to tour our facility. Our hard work was paying off and we were fast getting ready to add the energy conversion to our recycling plant.

To simplify the day-to-day operations, I had entered into a contracted relationship with a multi-billion dollar company that would provide me a percentage of the "net" profit if I allowed them to manage the overall project. Unfortunately, as much as I knew about science and engineering, I mistakenly trusted them on the distribution of the revenues. In our contract I had overlooked the wording and would receive only a net percentage of revenues of the overall project. I didn't realize the heart break and problems this oversight would cause. I had trusted them and found out later they knew exactly what they were doing.

They also encouraged me to travel to other locations to develop additional and similar projects all at my own expense. As I look back now, I can see they were hoping I would collapse under stress and financial strain.

In 1980, there became a great concern about a shortage of gasoline for our vehicles and interest turned to alcohol fuels. The debate back then was whether ethanol or methanol was better. Being interested in all types of alternative fuels, I attended a national conference in Ohio. The focus was on Bio-Mass to energy for use in cars. They called it Gas-Ahol, and most companies were focused on using corn. This brought me to my feet at the meeting and I

Joyce at the California Alcohol Fuel Conference.

stepped up to the microphone and said that we should be using all types of energy conversion to overcome our national fuel shortages. I also said that it's dangerous for the U.S. to be dependent on foreign oil. There are many waste products that could be converted to fuel.

Later, I was surprised to receive a Gas-Ahol news magazine with a picture of me at the microphone, with the comment below that it was pin-drop silence as I addressed the six hundred, almost all male audience members who represented many companies and governmental agencies. My picture and statement was a full-page article.

Another conference I attended in 1980, was held in California. This was a three-day international alternative fuels conference. While there I became quite well acquainted with engineers from several other countries, including those from Japan, South Africa, Germany, England, and India. They were very interested in my project with its unique cutting-edge technology. During our conversations, I was quite surprised to learn that some other countries were already using a variety of interesting energy conversion methods for bio-mass fuels. After further discussion, it became obvious that other nations were ahead of us in some of these areas and they wondered why the U.S. lagged behind.

Later, when I was back home, representatives from several municipalities and top companies in the U.S. contacted me. We met and discussed possible future projects in other areas needing to meet federal regulations for their waste disposal, as well as potential energy conversion plants.

A president of one of those large corporations invited me to

Kentucky to meet with him and his top expert engineers who were involved in many areas of all types of energy conversion and hazardous waste disposal.

He picked me up at the airport and drove to his office in a high-rise building. I was a little surprised as we walked into his office and saw there was a chair for me directly in front of his four seated engineers. I felt like I was in court and the engineers were judges. Each engineer was an expert in a certain field.

Their demeanor was like, "Who is this woman and what does she really know?" They began to ask me questions about various topics such as federal regulations for ocean dumping and reclamation, landfill containment to protect soil, aquifers and water ways. They questioned me about air quality control and waste heat boilers, verses pyrolysis, and how the heat would create steam turbines to generate electricity.

They questioned me about specific methods for coal gasification and a system that would extract oil from tar sand and oil shale. They questioned me about the feasibility of utilizing geo-thermal energy, explicit techniques concerning environmentally safe methods for hazardous waste disposal, and more in-depth questions about co-disposal of sewage sludge and solid waste, as well as the co-generation of steam and electricity without the use of fossil fuels.

Dr. Joyce, President of J.E. Hunt & Associates

Finally, after about three and a half hours, they took a break and said they would get back with me shortly. Within twenty minutes the president came back in, pulled a chair up beside me, and said, "Joyce, do you realize you're at least ten years ahead of anyone in our company. We look forward to working with you on a project."

After a few days of arriving back home, I received an official letter from them stating they recognized my expertise in the fields we had discussed of co-disposal, alternative energy and more. The president confirmed they were looking forward to working with me on a future project. Unfortunately, and unexpectedly, my circumstances changed and I was unable to follow up on these additional opportunities.

CHAPTER 21

SKULL FRACTURE

One night in December 1981, I felt a stabbing pain in my right eye. When I got up to see what the problem might be, I fell, hit my head, and later found out I'd fractured my skull in two places.

My eye issue was a scratched cornea, but the sight in my other eye was also threatened, due to my skull fracture.

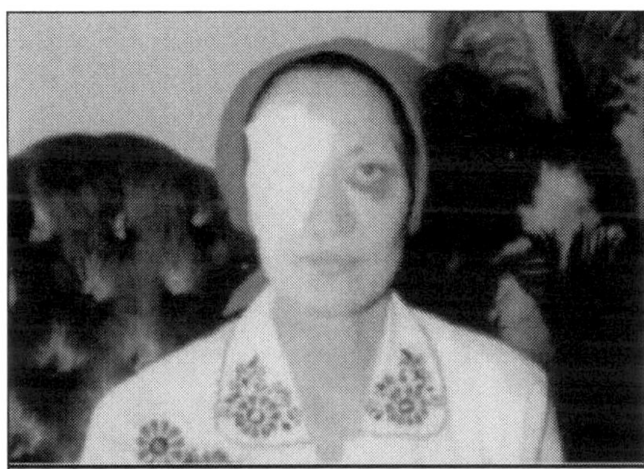

Joyce when she had a skull fracture and a scratched cornea (she almost lost her eye).

After a few days I recovered somewhat, and continued to keep in regular contact on the phone from my home office. No one on the project or my other associates were aware that I was injured.

I was able to coordinate final engineering construction and financing while using the phone for the 30 million-dollar energy conversion plant. In designing this project, I worked with top engineers from all over the globe, but especially with world-renowned, U.S. engineer Ellis Armstrong, who served as the Commissioner of the U.S. Bureau of Public Roads from 1958 to 1961, and oversaw the early development of President Dwight Eisenhower's Interstate Highway System.

The assigned agent from the large company I had contracted with who was supposed to be working for and on my behalf on my energy conversion project, would call me and come up with multiple reasons why I should not attend our monthly meetings with representatives from the county and the employees.

Gradually, I felt intimidated by their put-downs and sly comments. Perhaps I wasn't needed at the meetings anyway. The contract was definitely in my name and they told me I had nothing to worry about.

From the way they treated me, it became difficult to even be around them. Not realizing it at the time, with their subtle pressure and intimidation, I was developing a severe condition known as agoraphobia. It progressed to the point where I didn't want to leave the house and was reluctant to even be in small crowds.

Unbeknownst to me, the multi-billion dollar company that I had legally contracted with to work for me, used the time that I was not physically present, to advance their agenda of replacing my contract with their own.

The business was doing very well, but somehow my percentage of the profit was always small and was not covering my expenses.

One day as I was sitting at my desk in my home office, water dripped on my head. My roof was leaking. There was so much water damage it actually almost caved in. While I was dealing with all the business and personal issues and expenses, I fell again and broke my lower back and tailbone.

The despondency I had experienced in the past returned because of the physical and increasing financial problems I was experiencing.

With all of this weighing down on me, my thoughts went to when my father committed suicide in 1980.

I remember there were only a few people at his grave-side service. I listened as they discussed my father. They talked about how he had a successful detective agency, bought and sold real estate, and was a commercial building contractor of shopping malls and housing developments. I remember them saying how brilliant he was.

They discussed how he had become very wealthy with these businesses, but had a recent huge loss which was apparently so overwhelming, that it contributed to his decision to commit suicide.

I had sat staring at his steel, gray casket, vividly thinking that death could be the answer for me too. My leaking roof, recent fall, my own financial and health situations that I was facing, brought back to the surface my own thoughts of wanting to die again.

Also, what I didn't realize at the time was that I was beginning to suffer from a condition known as myasthenia gravis, an auto-immune disease. The muscle weakness I was experiencing led to more falls and more pain.

In mid-1982, I contracted pneumonia and upper respiratory infections and became allergic to the antibiotics. In addition, I was diagnosed with rheumatoid arthritis. I grew weaker, was in constant pain, and became bedridden. I just wanted to die.

When I was 49 years old, in January 1983, being still so ill and in so much pain, the doctor finally did some extensive tests.

Afterward he told me that I had an extremely low white blood cell count, my body's ability to heal was failing, and there was no hope for my recovery. With this news, I was sincerely more thrilled than someone would be if they had a winning lottery ticket. I was not going to have to end my life myself. I was just going to die and go to that place of peace that I wanted from the time I was a small child.

CHAPTER 22

NEAR-DEATH EXPERIENCE

One day after my condition worsened, I woke up feeling barely conscious, I realized death was approaching faster than I expected.

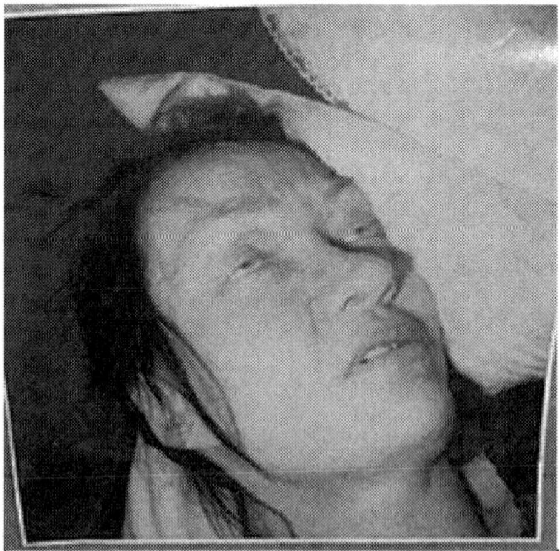

Snapshot taken by Crystal, my granddaughter, a few days before I went to the Other Side—January 1983.

Needing a little more time to get my burial plans arranged I dragged myself into the bathroom and leaning over the tub to be in a reverent position to pray, I wanted to ask God for just this small additional time.

As thoughts were forming in my mind to try to find the right words, I heard a voice that said, "If you come, you come now."

Instantly I was up, looking down at my body that had slumped over the edge into the tub.

Hovering in the air, I was a wispy being without a body. Realizing I had actually died, and was on the Other Side, I instantly felt shocked and amazed. Death was not what I expected it to be at all.

Death is not the end.

I personally discovered there *is* life after life. Knowledge flooded over me with a sharp reality. Words are inadequate to describe where I was, what happened, and what additional revelations were shown to me. I realized I was in a spiritual realm. I instantly knew that God is real!

[** My actuality of being in the presence of the bright, white light of God, and His Love, are shared from my heart to yours in the countless inspiring truths I learned while there in the Heavenly Realm. For more in-depth information and inspirational details about what the Other Side is like, as well as details of my near-death experience, be sure to read my companion book, *God's Heavenly Answers: Near-Death Experience Revealed.***]

I had a very extensive review of my life, including others' viewpoints, as well as God's perspective which is much higher than ours. I discovered *trying* counts, and God judges us by the intent of our hearts.

While I was alive, I'd always wondered why I didn't have a different, more loving and caring mother. We'd had many differences of opinions and arguments. Suddenly, I realized that she needed *me*. And I was so sorry for the times my words had hurt her.

I saw how much time I had wasted in my life arguing with other people over who was right and what was right. I saw that most everyone believed they were right and wanted others to know they were right. It really didn't matter. Most people have different memories of the same event.

During my life review, I saw how important it is to just let go, forgive, be quiet, and go on. The relationship is more important than who is right.

It reminded me of the parlor game where ten people sit in a circle and someone whispers a sentence in the first person's ear, who then quietly repeats the sentence to the next person, and so on. By the time it makes its way through each person in the circle, the sentence is totally different. Each person had good intentions of repeating it exactly, but it ends up sounding like an entirely different subject.

That's what happens with many people in our Earth lives, when we argue over previous events. It can be a futile waste of time that destroys relationships.

God judges the intent of our hearts. We shouldn't judge over foolish arguments and worry about who is right or wrong. Life is too short to be easily offended, angry and hold grudges. When we are thoughtful and kind, we are more apt to have loving and special relationships with family, friends, and business associates.

Ultimately, we need to be forgiving and as it says in the Bible in the Lord's Prayer, "Forgive us our trespasses, as we forgive others." This is an eternal truth, regardless of anyone's religious beliefs.

While on the Other Side, I was shown the importance of the Sermon on the Mount, and, as it says, "Blessed are the peace makers: for they shall be called the children of God." [Matthew 5:9, KJV]

I also learned the value of just listening, without judgment or providing a solution. Many people just need to talk and feel validated as someone listens. Whether they are right or wrong, they don't always want a solution, but just need to talk to someone and feel like someone cares. When we pray and tell our problems to God, He is an understanding listener. But we must also express gratitude and appreciation for the blessings we already have, and, in doing so, we may receive many miracles which we would not have otherwise received.

Whenever we feel a prompting, we should follow through, which could be for our own good, or others. Often, we could be the answer to someone's prayer. God usually answers our prayers through other people. We are more apt to have our own answers to prayers when we help others. For as we give, so shall we receive. Even if it's in the afterlife.

I felt horrendous regret for wasting so much valuable and limited Earth time, wanting to give up rather than learning and growing as I made it through life's problems and challenges. I essentially went through life with the attitude of a quitter. I lacked faith in a reason for living. Even though I understood the power of positive thinking, I didn't understand just how powerful our thinking is, or just how much our beliefs and our faith in God work together to create miracles. I had also bought into the popular myth that, just by dying, I would automatically receive an *unearned* peace. In other words, by lacking an eternal perspective, rather than realizing an *earned* peace and joy, I had brought on much of my own mental anguish and despair by my negative thinking and desire to give up.

It was revealed to me that our time on Earth in physical form allows us to do things that are not possible once we die, and that we are all given many opportunities to make our lives and the lives of those around us better.

I realized that when it is our time to go, we go home to whatever peace and celebration with family and friends that God has prepared for us. ("In my Father's house are many mansions."[John 14: 2, KJV]

Another great truth crashed in on me; had I died by my own hand, it would have caused great anguish to my loved ones and additional regret for me on the Other Side.

Suddenly, I heard a chorus of voices from those in the Spirit World who wanted to comfort their loved ones left behind on Earth, and especially those who were excessively grieving. They wanted to tell them that they are now their spiritual cheerleaders from the Other Side, to have faith, that God is real, and to move on with their lives and make the best use of their own limited Earth time.

I felt the hurtful awareness that I could no longer communicate to my loved ones on Earth. Anything I had not said could no longer be said. Anything I had not written, like a life history, could no longer be written. All of this, I had taken for granted. I discovered that a journal with lessons of life is a legacy you leave for family, friends, and others.

The awakening of my consciousness revealed how my Earth life experiences, including heartaches, physical hardships, and perceived roadblocks, were actually part of the learning and growth process of life.

Just as it states in Galatians 6:7, I personally learned that "Whatsoever a man soweth, that shall he also reap" is absolutely true. Even though it may not be during our life here on Earth.

Having been so trapped in my feelings of despair, despondency, and depression I had missed countless opportunities to perform acts of kindness and to help others who would have reaped eternal benefits.

All that mattered, I discovered, was what I did with the opportunities I had, and I was not measured against what I did not have or what anyone else did or did not do.

In addition, I became aware that our time begins counting down the day we are born. None of us know when our time will be over, not the day or the hour.

I learned the importance of forgiveness and that just as we want to be forgiven, we must forgive and be tolerant of others.

No longer did I want justice, as I had on Earth. I wanted *mercy*.

I discovered the importance of taking care of our mental and physical health, rather than being obsessed with the fads and fashions of the day. After my near-death experience, I was no longer anorexic or overly concerned about my weight.

My belief in God was replaced with an absolute *knowing* that He is real! I know from my own personal experience that the Scriptures are true and that God is filled with Love, Mercy, and Grace for us all. As I learned on the Other Side, this is true regardless of the name or title people use to refer to Him. Whether people call Him "God," "Lord," or "Higher Power," His answer to me and to all of us is: "I Am Who I Am."

There are many different religious teachings and faiths in the world. I suggest you keep looking until you know in your heart and soul, including through prayer, that you have found the truth of God.

I realized each one of us is to fulfill our own unique purpose for living on Earth, to learn and grow, to make it through problems, rather than giving up, repent and to prepare to meet God. I also learned that everyone is born during their own particular time in the world's history for a Divine purpose.

During this experience, I felt God's all-consuming unconditional love for me, mankind, and all of creation. I had never felt love like this and wanted to bask in it. I wished more than anything that I could share this feeling, especially with my loved ones and the *whole world*.

Words are inadequate to describe this immense feeling of God's love for me and each one of us.

I felt like an unbelievably large wave of heavenly and earthly knowledge swept over me. Our bodies are electric and everything that we think, eat, or drink, affects our physical well-being. Our words and especially our thoughts create energy that influences our mind, body and spirit. These can interrupt or improve our direct line to Heaven.

While on the Other Side, the horrendous regrets and agonizing mental anguish I felt by giving up on life were much worse than any physical pain I had while alive on Earth.

One other very important lesson loomed large: *miracles are possible for everyone*, especially for those who believe in them. All my priorities changed. I was a transformed person.

Even though it seemed useless, I pleaded with God for another chance to live. I promised, if I could live again, I would share with everyone who would listen to God's messages, the importance of helping others, and using precious limited Earth time wisely.

Every part of my being pleaded with God, "Oh please, let me have another chance to live!" Though it seemed the answer was "no," with all my heart, I continued to plead and beg.

CHAPTER 23

MY FAMOUS GOLD-CROWNED TOOTH

While on the Other Side, suddenly, I saw in my mind's eye a large image of one of my gold-crowned teeth. I'd had the crown for over fifteen years and knew exactly which tooth this was in the upper right quadrant. While it had never given me pain, God revealed to me that it was a major source of many of my health problems. The dangers and health problems caused by amalgam fillings (which are 50% mercury) was also revealed to me.

As quickly as I had left my body, I found myself back in it, slumped over the tub. I lifted my hands and could once again feel my face. I was not that wispy being anymore. I had a new awareness that this Earth world is not actually the *real* world. Then, somehow, I managed to drag my exhausted body back into bed.

After having had my life review on the Other Side, which was filled with so many regrets, I knew that the next time I die I want to have Heavenly peace of mind while in God's presence.

However, I was surprised when I had returned to my body with another chance to live. Thinking back over my life review, I realized then, that *anything* I had *previously repented for* while I was alive, was not included in my afterlife review. Mistakes that I had felt terrible about, but had repented of, were *gone*.

I also realized that I had a new purpose for living with an eternal perspective, and the way for me to have this peace of mind would be to share these truths so others can find their true purpose for living.

With the miracle of another chance to live, I now wanted to savor every moment of life to the fullest. I knew any problems I would encounter were meant for my growth.

As soon as I could muster enough strength, I made an appointment with my dentist, Dr. Richard Smart, DDS. I told him about my vision of the tooth during my Other Side experience, and requested that he pull it immediately. He asked me if the tooth hurt, and I said no. He then took an x-ray and said it showed nothing wrong. But I adamantly insisted that the tooth needed to be pulled.

Joyce back from the afterlife and grateful to be alive.

He was so reluctant that in order to pull it he insisted I would need to sign a legal paper releasing him from all liability for extracting what he believed to be a perfectly healthy tooth. After I signed the document, he arranged an appointment with an oral surgeon.

As soon as the tooth was out, the surprised oral surgeon held it out in front of me where we could both obviously see its blackened, decomposed roots which had led to a bad infection up through my jaw and into my sinuses.

Within a couple of days, I took my removed tooth back to show Dr. Smart. He requested permission and cut it in half. It had a large amount of mercury-silver amalgam under the gold-crown.

With the tooth removed, I started to feel better immediately. In addition, it felt like pins and needles were coming out of every pore of my body for several days, as whatever was in my system seemed to be working its way out.

The tooth had contained silver amalgam (mercury) as well as gold, and had apparently been causing inflammation in my body that had prevented my upper respiratory infections from healing.

Within the next several days, I went to a dentist and had all of my silver amalgam (mercury) fillings removed. Within about three weeks I felt much better and my painful arthritis was all but gone.

It is now my belief that teeth with infections, root canals, and especially silver mercury fillings are the *root cause* of many of the illnesses that are almost impossible to diagnose. Over the years, I became more aware of the problems these fillings can cause. I also learned that when these fillings are removed, for their disposal, they have to go into a container that is sent to a *hazardous waste facility.*

I agree with many top holistic medical professionals that there is a great lack of knowledge in dentistry and its connection with our physical health. Warning: We only get the care that the doctor or dentist has had the training and background to provide.

A new trend for doctors, health specialists, and others is towards *functional medicine.* There are benefits and cautions depending on the depth of the practitioner's training.

Without question, I firmly believe that when one has a lingering illness it is wise to seek *holistic* doctors and *holistic* dentists to find the best health solutions.

Also, I believe it is vitally important to obtain thermographic images of the head and body which will show inflammation. The best thermography camera I've found is the Medi-Therm. It is FDA approved. This is not the same type that is used for detecting heat in buildings; this is an entirely different technology.

By using the medical thermographic camera, an *adequately trained* holistic practitioner can usually tell where any inflammation exists in the head or body, which can be a sign of infection or other problems. Numerous times with patients with whom I've worked, it was an infected tooth or multiple teeth that was taking their immune system down.

After the infected teeth were pulled, their health improved, sometimes dramatically, and they had more energy than they'd had in years. Usually, people don't realize to what degree problems with their teeth and gums can affect their general health or even *cause* disease. In fact, my dying and going to the Other Side was caused by a bad tooth.

Despite my own personally transforming near-death experience, I readily admit that I was quite relieved when I first learned of Sam Ziff's 1984 book, *Silver Dental Fillings: The Toxic Time Bomb: Can the Mercury in Your Dental Fillings Poison You?* I no longer felt like a lone wolf in wanting to share the potential

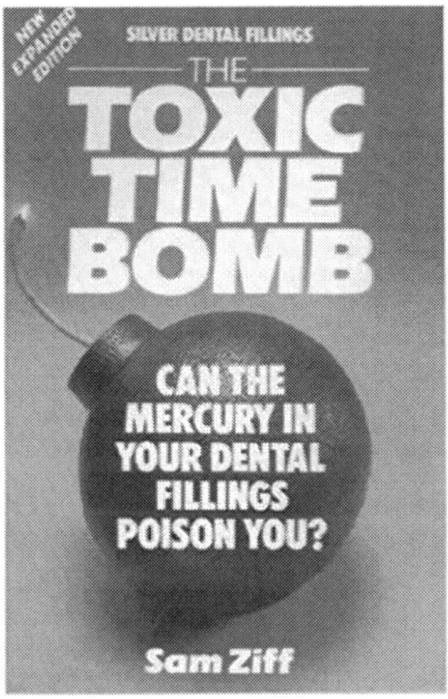

dangers of mercury amalgam fillings. Today, fortunately, the FDA is now acknowledging the potential harm of "mercury-containing" amalgam. The FDA's September 24, 2020 press release, entitled "FDA Issues Recommendations for Certain High-Risk Groups Regarding Mercury-Containing Dental Amalgam," does contain certain qualifiers, but it's an important admission nonetheless, and, moreover, they do explicitly include "people with [a] pre-existing neurological disease such as multiple sclerosis, Alzheimer's disease or Parkinson's disease."

There are considerable potential advantages of getting the amalgam fillings removed—not least of which is helping your immune system. Rather than battling the effects of the release of mercury vapor (from eating food, chewing gum, or grinding your teeth), your immune system can concentrate on whatever else your body may be dealing with. If you do have your mercury amalgam filings removed, however, be sure to have the procedure done by a dentist trained in the proper protocol, including using a "dental dam" to prevent any of the mercury particles from sliding down your throat and into your stomach.

People, understandably, often complain to me about the costs of removing amalgam fillings. Depending on the person's health condition, and financial situation, I occasionally feel compelled to remind some of them, "It's cheaper than a funeral!"

When I first returned to Earth life, I still had pain from the failed back surgeries, but my feelings of self-condemnation had been completely replaced with gratitude for life. Also, the appreciation I had acquired for being back in my body made the pain and discomfort bearable.

After struggling with depression for years, feeling now a new purpose for living, I had also *conquered depression and any thoughts of suicide.*

I was committed to using the knowledge I had gained to live a better life and to help others. I accepted that I was meant to leave that other world behind, to be back in my physical body, and had a strong desire to live and to meet head on whatever was put in front of me.

What had helped me get through life so far was prayers, miracles, *sleep learning*, determined willpower and positive affirmations. However, it was not until my near-death experience that I realized and understood that my purpose for living was working *through* problems rather than giving up because of them.

I discovered that suicide is not the answer, and what is important is to be grateful, loving, kind, forgiving, and merciful.

These things feed the human soul, and as you learn how to draw on the powers of heaven in the pages ahead you will find many additional answers for your own earthly challenges.

Still, there were many challenges ahead in my own life.

CHAPTER 24

A CAREER-CHANGING LAWSUIT

Love came into my life and I married Earl Brown in December of 1983. After he retired as an air force major, he became Senior Vice President for Farm Credit Bank. We met and married while he was President of Producer's Livestock Marketing. Our future looked bright. He was a widower and had a very special family. Interestingly, I still think of some of them every year on their birthdays. I also remember seeing a picture of Earl when he was in the service with the chest of his uniform covered in medals. He served in World War II, the Korean War, and Vietnam.

Although there were many positives, unexpectedly, in the spring of 1984, Earl had a major heart attack which brought on serious health problems and great challenges. The doctors said that he only had weeks to live and could die of a major heart attack at any time.

Utilizing holistic health care treatments, he totally improved—so much so that he went back to work for the place where he had retired.

Making sure he got the care and treatments he needed, it critically divided my time as a caregiver and busy professional business owner.

In 1984 and 1985, it became a confusing series of battles to maintain control of the energy conversion contract.

Suddenly, in 1986, I realized that the agents from my alternative energy business, rather than working on my behalf, had instead been trying to cut me out of the profits. They also attempted to eliminate me from the business entirely by trying to replace my long-term government contract with their own.

In early spring of 1986, I received a letter from a Fortune 500 company recognizing my personal expertise in waste-to-energy, recycling, pollution control and hazardous waste disposal. Also, in this letter they guaranteed performance and financing for my multi-million dollar project. It would produce megawatts of electricity, pollution free, for the power company, replacing coal.

But it was too late.

An official representative of the large company I had hired arranged to meet with me and I was expecting to receive a check for $250,000 for the net revenue for the past year. I was surprised and thrilled by this amount since it was, by far, the largest I'd ever received from the project.

Instead, I was shocked when he informed me the corporation was no longer honoring my contract with them. They had closed down the plant, laid off the employees, and made arrangements for a landfill company to take over the facility. However, instead of giving me a check, he told me I would have to retain an attorney and file a lawsuit in order to get my money.

I retained an attorney, and a lawsuit was filed. I did not realize at the time that court cases were full of unexpected delays, that almost always drag out for many years, and that *justice* and *fairness* is most often found only in the dictionary. The large company I was fighting had deep pockets, hired several top attorneys dedicated to this case, and the resulting lawsuit dragged on and on.

After years and extremely high legal fees, and the requirement for me to add additional specialized attorneys who were also to be paid from the settlement, some information surfaced to support my case. A possible settlement was mentioned, but nothing came of it.

The lawsuit also caused stress to my husband. It was demanding more and more of my time and attention to deal with all the details of the case. This just added to the daily challenges.

As I underwent the ordeal of the lawsuit, the stress was causing my muscles to weaken. I also had problems with breathing.

The energy I had to sustain my life was slowly being sapped. The huge financial burdens, the loss of my project, including future income, and the entanglements involved by being in a multi-million dollar lawsuit, caused me to almost crash. I felt devastated.

One day, I collapsed and literally fell to my knees. With heartfelt sorrow, as tears rolled down my cheeks, I prayed harder than ever before for inspiration, guidance, and a miracle.

Critically, I realized I needed even stronger and more powerfully worded *sleep learning* recordings to help me get control of my thinking, feelings, and actions. I knew that a professional recording studio and special equipment would be required to make this happen.

In 1987, this project became a reality. I produced revolutionary and unique *sleep learning* recordings using Super-Subliminals™ with positive affirmations.

After they were produced, listening to them helped me go into a deeper level of sleep, rest more, concentrate better, feel calmer, and have more confidence during extremely stressful situations.

The results produced were miraculous. Since then I have transferred these recordings to digital to make them compatible with present day technology and available to others.

CHAPTER 25

WARNING SIGNS OVERLOOKED

At this point, my muscle weakness persisted. I had problems walking and had to wear a neck brace to hold my head up, plus an ankle brace. Previously, I had been making excuses, saying, "I just need to exercise more," or "I've been under a lot of stress."

I started having muscle cramps and muscle twitching. The twitching worsened day by day. I felt like I had something bouncing around under my skin. I later learned these were called fasciculations.

Other symptoms that I had for the past couple of years, such as difficulty swallowing and breathing, as well as dropping things, became more pronounced and serious. I began to severely choke on my own saliva. My eyelids were badly drooping. To make matters worse, I had lost most of my voice. People had difficulty understanding me and I was embarrassed and reluctant to speak and have conversations.

ALS DIAGNOSIS

Although I was frightened and tried to deny these symptoms, I knew I needed to find out what was wrong. In May of 1988, I sought the help of Dr. Willem Khoe, a renowned medical doctor who also practiced homeopathy, acupuncture and traditional Chinese medicine in Las Vegas, Nevada.

He diagnosed me with myasthenia gravis (MG), but told me that some of my symptoms were not consistent with it, and that I also had ALS, amyotrophic lateral sclerosis, or Lou Gehrig's disease. Because of my problems breathing, he immediately gave me a prescription to be on oxygen.

The myasthenia gravis (MG) had masked many of my ALS symptoms. Some of the symptoms are similar, but ALS has additional symptoms that are totally different. As an example, muscles may weaken, but do not atrophy with MG, as they do with ALS.

Dr. Khoe was the first medical professional to diagnose me with ALS. At the time, I had no idea what it was. Even though MG is also a potentially life-threatening disease, and I still have to take medication for it regularly, he said that he could only focus on the ALS.

Despite my doubts, I trusted Dr. Khoe and agreed to the weekly treatments. He ordered the remedies and we started the treatments the following week.

When I went home, I researched ALS and found there were about 5,000 new cases per year in the United States, and about 220,000 worldwide. I became extremely frightened. Could Dr. Khoe possibly be wrong?

This disease appeared to be fatal, and have no cure. I was only in my fifties. I thought to myself, "Is this why I went to the 'Other Side', so I could die from ALS?"

Deciding I wanted a second opinion, I went to a very knowledgeable and experienced Naturopathic Physician. He performed various tests and also concluded that I had ALS.

Even though I had all these scary symptoms, doubts still plagued my mind. I just could not accept that I had this paralyzing, fatal disease. In order to be sure that my diagnosis was correct, in June of 1988 I sought out a third doctor. This one was a neurologist who had experience with ALS at a clinic in Salt Lake City, Utah.

He confirmed the diagnosis, and said, "You're doing very well for the stage you're in. Stick out your tongue and you will see that you cannot hold it still. You should make it to Thanksgiving."

As I stuck out my quivering tongue, I realized he was right. I had been in total denial. Thanksgiving was a mere five months away. I was 54 years old.

Not knowing what else to do, I began going to ALS support groups. The first one I attended was in Utah. The message was clear: "Do whatever you want, because you're going to die anyway. It doesn't matter what you think or what doctor you go to, because nothing can be done."

During a trip to southern California, I found another support group. Again, the talk was negative: "You're going to die, so just accept it." I thought, "No wonder people lost hope of recovering from this disease."

The one thing I did know was that if I were going to get better, it would not be by being around people who think like *this!*

CHAPTER 27

AN ANSWER TO PRAYERS

Having been to the Other Side, I knew there was hope for a miracle.

When I had previously gone to Dr. Khoe, he told me about a treatment from Germany for ALS. He said that a remarkable number of the people who were given a special homeopathic remedy recovered.

Unfortunately, Dr. Khoe passed away in 1992, and I have not yet been able to find an equivalent homeopathic remedy.

In America, there were no known survivors that I knew about. Years later, I found out there actually was an ALS survivor. Her name is Evy McDonald. Dr. Khoe had told me he could not make any promises, but at this point, I felt I had nothing to lose, and that's why I decided to go ahead with the treatment.

The homeopathic remedy was mixed with my own blood, and then injected into specific acupuncture points. I agreed to try a course of one shot a week for ten weeks, even though I had to travel about 900 miles round trip to Las Vegas each time I received a treatment. My mother was kind enough to accompany me. It made the long trips go by faster.

During one of my early visits to Dr. Khoe in Las Vegas, I attended an ALS support group there.

In Utah and California, neurologists ran the meetings, documented each person's worsening conditions, cut off anyone who had a positive story to share and instead told patients what to expect as the disease progressed towards death.

In Nevada, it was a very different experience. The ALS patients complained that they rarely got to see a neurologist. The meetings were conducted by a social worker.

What surprised me as an observer was that the ALS patients in the Nevada group seemed to be living years longer than either the Utah or the California group. In the Nevada group, all of them *walked* by themselves into the meeting even though, on

63

average, it was years longer since their diagnosis than either of the other two groups, most of whom were already in wheelchairs or used scooters.

To this day, I have no doubt that it was because there was no neurologist telling them how soon they were going to die. In addition, instead of listening to patients list their worsening conditions to the neurologist, the Nevada ALS patients shared more of what they were doing that gave them motivation to live.

At this point, I decided not to attend ALS support groups anymore. There was nothing there that was going to help me. In fact, I felt it was discouraging.

Instead, I focused on getting well and not allowing any negative thoughts to enter my mind.

I continued the homeopathic treatment as well as prayer, maintaining a relentlessly positive mental attitude and consistently listening to *sleep learning* and meditating daily.

During treatment, Dr Khoe advised me to stop consuming meat products due to the hormones and antibiotics the animals were given. At the time, I did not believe that what I ate made much difference, so after one treatment I went right out to the nearest fast-food place and had a huge double cheeseburger!

Not long after this incident, driving home with my mom from Las Vegas, we parked our RV at a truck stop next to a big field. The following morning, I awoke to loud mooing and a terrible odor coming from a huge cattle truck parked right next to us—despite *all* of the many other open spaces where he could have parked. The cows were staring straight at me, accusingly, through the holes and bars of their mobile prison.

At that moment I remembered my doctor's advice about not eating meat, and decided to give it up then and there during the treatments. Those poor cows really got my attention! To me, this was a clear message from God.

I improved my diet, continued to pray, and listened to my recorded positive affirmations during the day and *sleep learning* at night. These recordings helped reduce the tremendous stress I was under. I knew it was important to stay positive.

Still, I had doubts. It was becoming harder and harder to walk. My choking got so bad I was embarrassed to eat in public. I even thought I might die from choking before the ALS had a chance to kill me.

My voice deteriorated to the point that I knew if it got much worse I would need something to communicate with others, so I looked for a voice board so people could point to a word or letter and I could acknowledge yes or no by blinking my eyes.

Around this time my lawsuit was still in progress, but my doctors sent notes to the court that because of my condition after my ALS diagnosis I was unable to withstand the stress of depositions or testimony.

Had I been forced to testify at this time, I was certain the stress would have killed me. (Later, when my deposition was taken, it lasted *many* very stressful days.)

After the 10 weeks of homeopathic treatments, and 9000 miles of driving, I saw only mild improvements. I certainly didn't feel cured by the end of it. What now? If the remedy was going to work, the ALS should have been on the way out by now.

Then Dr. Khoe went on vacation, I missed my homeopathic injection that week and we both noticed I didn't do as well without it. After talking with him, he agreed to let me have the shots for a few more weeks.

Meanwhile, I kept on praying, but with even greater frequency and intensity. I also continued to listen to and mentally recite positive affirmations throughout the day so that I could better control my thoughts, feelings and actions.

After praying with a close friend and believer, we were left with the strong conviction that, in this particular case, it was my choice whether I would live or die. I was praying to live and doing my best to make it so. In addition, I prepared myself spiritually in case God had other plans for me.

In the prayer, I was also told if I decided to live, God was going to bless my voice. For someone in my compromised physical condition who lost their voice, this seemed hard to believe. Still, I prayed that it was true.

One day, a few days after receiving my last shot of the homeopathic remedy, during a sincere heartfelt prayer, I felt something change.

I remember it was as if a light gray smoke had lifted up off me.

A short while later my husband stated that "something was different" about me, and I seemed better. I sensed it too. I felt stronger and the choking stopped.

Immediately, I felt improvement in many ways, and in the coming weeks I noticed my muscle wasting stopped its progression.

My doctor gave me some tests. Afterwards, he declared that my ALS was gone.

It was a miracle.

My energy and strength quickly returned to normal.

The choking episodes and muscle twitching completely stopped.

After more time, my voice fully recovered, and even now at almost 90 years old, I am often mistaken on the phone for a much younger person.

CHAPTER 28

A LETTER FROM DR. LOGAN

While writing this book, I had a conversation with Dr. Logan, who was one of my three doctors during my ALS recovery. I am including his letter here as part of my story.

February 12, 2021

To Whom It May Concern:

Joyce has been a patient of mine over many years. I am unable to find her original file, but it was around the early 1980s when I first saw her. In the later part of the 1980s, having treated her before she was ill, I became aware of changes in her complaints, symptoms, and physical condition. She had weakness, muscle atrophy, choking problems, and loss of most of her voice. She was also on oxygen because of her breathing problems. I did some tests and it appeared she had ALS.

Dr. Willem Khoe, MD, in Las Vegas also diagnosed ALS for Joyce. I have met him and knew that he had used some alternative medical techniques that worked well for her. My findings and additional neurologists Joyce had seen were consistent with Dr. Khoe's diagnoses that she was in an advanced stage of ALS.

I saw Joyce soon after she completed her treatments with Dr. Khoe and she had none of her former ALS complaints or symptoms.

To this day, even at age 87, she has the voice of a much younger person and leads an extremely active life. She is an author of several books, speaker, founder and president of Stress and Grief Relief, Inc., a non-profit organization for suicide prevention, including a life-saving hotline. Her website is www.hopedr.org.

This letter is to verify my personal knowledge of over thirty years of Joyce Brown's medical history, including her battle with ALS in 1988. I trust this will help with the direction of Joyce's present research into understanding this disease and the giving of hope to those who are searching for answers.

Sincerely yours,

Cordell E. Logan, Ph.D., ND.

CHAPTER 29

THE ALS REVERSAL RECIPE THAT WORKED FOR ME

People often ask me what things I did to reverse ALS, and what I do now if I have health problems. I believe that the miraculous healing of my ALS in 1988 was a combination of the following:

1. Prayer and a sincere personal relationship with God

2. Removal of all of the amalgam fillings (i.e. mercury and silver) from my teeth

3. Skilled homeopathy and acupuncture

4. A major change of diet, including striving to eat organic, giving up non-grass-fed meat, and drinking adequate amounts of filtered water.

5. *Belief* that I could heal, which was profoundly influenced by my near-death experience

6. Listening to my *sleep learning* recordings *Whispers for Life & Prosperity*, and *Whispers for Miraculous Results* (see image below), which gave me a positive attitude towards life and increased my own body's ability to heal, and

7. A specialized, personalized meditation using the CD of *Whispers for Miraculous Results*.

As a result of decades of study and experience, I have found there are great health benefits from these additional practices:

1. A doctor that can administer an intravenous (IV) of vitamins and minerals, especially one that is high in Vitamin C and Glutathione.

2. A physician trained to use ozone therapy that increases the oxygen in the blood in order to build the immune system.

3. Deep breathing of pure, clean air.

4. Increase the body's healing energy, which is affected by what we eat, drink, and think, including prayer, but also how we are impacted by the energy in our environment, including how well we manage stress.

This is my personal basic recipe that I have recommended. However, there is additional information that is helping others with reversals at: <u>HealingALS.org</u>.

CHAPTER 30

A MIRACULOUS HEALING

Though three doctors had diagnosed me, and the symptoms are easily found on the internet, I have always been reluctant to talk about having had ALS, let alone the story of my miraculous recovery—that is, until now, when numerous others are telling about their ALS reversals.

When I wrote my book, *God's Heavenly Answers*, I only referred to my ALS as the broader group of diseases known as *Muscular Dystrophy*. At the time, no one else I knew of was talking about healing ALS, and I didn't want to be the first, nor did I want that to become the focus of my book.

One day in September of 2014, Patricia Tamowski called from New York and told me that she and her husband, Scott Douglas, were professional filmmakers. They were interviewing people who had ALS reversals and wanted to hear my story of recovery.

After asking her if I was the first one she had found, and learning I was the tenth, I agreed to share my personal experience. Patricia and Scott found out about me after tracking down an acquaintance of mine, a male in his forties who was also healed of ALS.

There was no way of knowing at the time what a great relationship would develop between us. In the beginning, I still found it very difficult to talk about. But shortly after Patricia contacted me, I started to open up. I gave Patricia permission to share my number with people who had ALS, and wanted to call and ask me questions, but I still felt slightly uncomfortable.

One day while sitting at the table in the kitchen thinking about not wanting to talk about my ALS experience, I suddenly heard a distinct voice say,

"I helped you!"

Instantly, a feeling swept over my whole body; I felt a deep sense of gratitude for being healed of ALS. I immediately felt a new desire to share my experience, and what I believe could help

71

others, with the hope and possibility that they too could have a miraculous healing. I now had a new desire, and a deeper awareness of the importance of sharing my story with people who have ALS.

Dr. Joyce with the other ALS speakers (all ALS reversals!)

CHAPTER 31

SHARING MY ALS STORY

Over the next few years Patricia and Scott came to my home to film, take pictures, and interview me about the various life-and-death adventures and miracles of my life. They even took a video of me dancing the twist with Scott (see photo below) showing how I had no after-effects from the ALS. This was also the time I was elated to see both Patricia and Scott at my public speaking competition where I was the International Toastmasters award-winning contestant for Southern Utah in 2018 at age 84. The title of my speech was, "Life is Worth Living." Meanwhile, they continued to gather information, and conduct interviews, many of which are published on their YouTube channel Healing Advocates.

Dr. Joyce dancing "The Twist" with Scott Douglas.

Patricia and Scott found other people who had healed from ALS, as well as those who were in different stages of the disease who needed hope and help. During their research they became acquainted with Richard Bedlack, M.D., Ph.D., Director of Duke University's ALS Clinic. As part of his research at Duke, Dr. Bedlack tracks and documents ALS reversals and, at present, has *confirmed* approximately 50 ALS reversals around the world. If you are interested in learning more about ALS reversals, I highly recommend you get in touch with Patricia and Scott who are currently learning about even more ALS reversals.

Since I started writing this book, I have learned of another

12 ALS reversals attributed to prayer, as well as 5 others attributed to homeopathy. This is exciting news and we are expecting to hear of many additional ALS reversals soon.

When Dr. Bedlack's colleague contacted me, requesting information about my medical history and recovery from ALS and having myasthenia gravis (MG), I was interested to learn from him that, even though it is rare, many of the ALS cases that he was studying also had MG.

After considerable organizing, preparation and pre-work, Patricia and Scott hosted the world's first ever Healing ALS Conference from the 18th to the 20th of October 2019 (www.HealingALSConference.org).

The 2019 Healing ALS Conference graphic, designed by Steve Arscott, a beloved member of the ALS community (diagnosed in 2013).

Held at the Radisson Hotel in Downtown Salt Lake City, the event was a spectacular success. Nearly 300 people attended the conference from over 10 different countries. The conference was also live-streamed to more than 25 nations around the world, with nearly 1,000 people tuning in.

It was a great privilege to be one of eight speakers with a complete reversal of ALS at the conference, and to share my life story of how I was miraculously healed in 1988. My slide presentation included pictures from my near-death experience, and my book, *God's Heavenly Answers*, as well as my *sleep learning* recordings with their powerful positive affirmations, *Whispers for Miraculous Results*. As I pointed out

in my speech, along with the steps I outlined earlier, I believe the recordings were a tremendously important part of my healing.

Knowing that the audience was filled with people who had ALS, as well as their caregivers, family, and friends, my heart was so touched that, as I shared my story, I could not hold back my tears.

I couldn't see them; however, it was as if I could personally feel their heartaches and challenges. Many were in power chairs, and differing stages of ALS. There was even one wife pushing her husband in a wheeled gurney, because he was too advanced with ALS to be able to sit up.

The audience from the Healing ALS Conference, including 300 in-person attendees and live-streamed to another 3,000 people in 30 countries around the world. Dr. Joyce is seated on stage speaking about her complete reversal from ALS back in 1988.

As the first Healing ALS conference, it was the only place in the world where there was hope and healing information available, as well as selected experts and top doctors who were there to share valuable information about ALS. I felt very grateful to have been healed of ALS in 1988, and I was honored to be there to share my story and offer hope that others can receive miracles too.

Since that conference, phone calls, letters and emails have been coming in continuously from people all over the world, who are advancing toward ALS reversal after what they learned. For more information about the conference and priceless information from leading experts in the field about health and healing, go to their website www.HealingALS.org.

We are also receiving letters and emails from people sharing their own success stories and miraculous results from using our unique coping techniques, *sleep learning* and other life-changing, life-saving information.

To learn more about the methods I personally used, go to our website www.HopeDr.org. You will also find life-changing books, articles, positive, stress relieving affirmations, recordings that help you learn while you sleep, meditations and so much more. Additionally, you will find information about how to have hope, reap miracles, and find relief from stress, depression and grief.

Still today, knowing that people need help and answers *now*, I feel a great urgency to make my books and recordings available as quickly as possible.

CHAPTER 32

CREATING MIRACULOUS RESULTS

Due to the fact that I have serious spinal issues, I only have so much time each day before I need to lie down. In addition to having visual impairment, these challenges make whatever miraculous results I'm striving for more complicated and time consuming.

I wholeheartedly believe that many different ailments I've recovered from and the calamities I've conquered over the years were influenced by my positive, purposeful, mentally programmed *belief* that I *would* recover, and furthermore, that I had not yet finished my real purpose for living.

Since my near-death experience, and personally knowing to whom I am praying, my prayers are now much deeper, more like a two-way conversation, as I listen for whisperings of the Spirit.

Whenever I think about what I might have done differently, looking back on my life and my ordeal with ALS, I wish I had picked up on and paid attention to my symptoms sooner—warning signs which had been going on far longer than I realized. However, considering all the stress I was under with the lawsuit, the symptoms seemed insignificant compared to everything else that was happening.

I now encourage others to take quick action when they sense that something is not right with their health, but also to have courage, faith, pray, and listen for promptings and direction from above.

Heavenly whisperings and interventions work differently for different people, although listening is always key.

During my near-death experience, I received guidance about my infected gold-crowned tooth with its silver fillings containing mercury.

Some people receive information and promptings with soft whisperings of the Spirit during prayers, reading scriptures, through dreams or simply by talking with others, or even by consulting with various specialists.

I should have been more in-tune with my own health, gone to see a specialist sooner, and changed my diet. Even now, when I stray too far from eating the right foods, I pay for it with health challenges, and have to get myself back in line.

I have found, in both my personal and professional experience, that many people who choose not to rely solely on the traditional medical establishment, tend to live healthier and longer lives.

While the conventional medical community is needed for many injuries and illnesses, looking outside of it allowed me to find the help that ultimately healed me.

Again, I'd like to emphasize the specific areas that I focused on, and have found most helpful for hope and healing, including the following: prayer, finding a purpose for living, homeopathy, along with acupuncture, holistic dentistry and getting amalgam fillings removed and replaced properly, listening to positive affirmations while you sleep, positive thinking and overall changing my attitude towards life, stress relief, with meditation, a healthy diet, and proper rest and exercise. Different things work for different people and their particular conditions, these are the main things that worked for me.

Often, I am asked to share the 2 or 3 most important factors on this list, however in my mind, all these suggestions rank number one.

My beliefs are based on my education and experience as a Naturopathic Doctor, working with renowned medical experts and scientists, as well as my personal knowledge with my own health and other people I have helped.

Holistic medicine takes work and research. Carrying out various protocols can be intense. At times working with a holistic MD and a nutritional specialist is invaluable. It is worth it though, for all the extra years of having loved ones in our lives, and the increased health and quality of life during those years.

If you go to a doctor or health specialist you aren't comfortable with, keep searching for a practitioner who shares your outlook, and helps you achieve the best possible results. Every doctor has his or her own training and perspective.

In addition, based on my observations, support groups which permit participants to share positive experiences and support one another seem to have better outcomes.

In 1988, the only option I knew about was to attend a group which focused on death, dying, and decline. Our present group, *Healing ALS,* with Patricia and Scott, inspires, encourages, and enlightens with a focus on hope and healing as well as sharing stories of successful ALS reversals.

For additional facts and information, as well as the most recent accounts, visit their website www.HealingALS.org.

The site is a storehouse of wisdom, knowledge and stories of peoples' improvements and ALS reversals, including my own account (see Dr. Joyce Brown's ALS Reversal Story Part 1, and Dr. Joyce Brown Q&A Part 2). Also, on You Tube are several videos under Dr. Joyce Brown Suicide Prevention. Other videos may be found on the website HopeDr.org as you browse the menu or use our search tool.

When asked why I was permitted to have another chance to live after my near-death experience, and why I didn't die from ALS when so many other good and deserving people have lost their lives, I can only say that I don't know.

Perhaps, at that time, I had not yet fulfilled my purpose here on Earth. We do not always know what God's plans are for each of us. If someone has done everything they can possibly do for their own health, if they are treating others with kindness and forgiveness, and if they are living the best they can each day, then it makes sense to make peace with their family and themselves, make the most of each moment, and trust God's will.

Even with sincere and repeated prayers, answers do not always come quickly or easily. Our timing and God's timing are not always the same. Sometimes it takes weeks, months, or even years of prayers to get the answer or miracle we seek.

When a miracle is needed, the road can be long and difficult before we feel we are connected and have a direct line to heaven.

Yet, often when we least expect it, we can receive a miraculous answer to our prayers directly from God. I know this firsthand, and if it happened for me, *I know it can happen for anyone.*

CHAPTER 33

AFTER ALS

After my recovery from ALS, I still had the lawsuit to contend with, which required an enormous amount of my attention. The court case dragged on with tremendous pressure from all of their attorneys.

After all that I had been going through, other health problems surfaced, and the stress was causing my myasthenia gravis (MG) symptoms to worsen.

I realized I needed to move on from a battle that was threatening my health and life.

To improve my health, and my life, I decided to forgo compensation for my losses, and in 1992, I accepted a settlement that barely covered the legal fees.

The worst part was the heartbreak of knowing that the 500 tons per day of solid waste garbage, *including plastic bags, bottles, and straws*, was no longer going to be converted to energy in my plant. Instead, it would be dumped into the landfill. Because of tradition and convenience, and because what is right and good does not always prevail, this process of putting most of the waste into landfills, versus converting it to energy, continues in most areas to this day.

It really hurt to leave behind that part of my life working in the alternative energy and hazardous waste fields. It was very depressing to know that there are solutions for pollution control and energy shortages that are not being implemented.

With the court case lasting six years, I felt overwhelmed and just wanted to become a different person. After all of those years of being in court with our lawsuit, so many financial losses, and dealing with attorney's, I felt extremely victimized.

When they breached the contract, laid off employees and left my project in about May of 1986, I quickly realized I needed to change fields and begin a whole new way of life.

No longer being able to help cities or counties, I decided I would focus on helping individuals with their spiritual, mental, and health issues. I realized this would require new intense studies, spiritual guidance, and miracles. I became deeply and actively engrossed in learning about the vast field of holistic health.

After God answered my pleadings with another chance to live, as I promised Him, my soul's sincere desire was to help people so they will enjoy the Other Side when they get there.

The lawsuit itself, however, was also turning out to be a tremendous learning experience. Five and a half years into it, facing some seventeen different attorneys in court, I decided I wanted to learn more about the law. In fact, I developed a deep desire to know more about the legal world which surrounds us.

After making a few inquiries, an associate suggested I check with the University of West Los Angeles Law School for more information. I knew I didn't have the time, energy, or money to go to law school, but I wanted to learn more about the bigger picture, so I called and asked if they had any courses available that I could take to learn about the legal system. I was quite surprised when they told me of a 5-week "post graduate" program that they were about to launch as part of their Professional Advancement Series. They billed the series of concentrated lectures—covering everything from contracts, torts, and wills to legal research, judicial process, and criminal law—as a "mini law school," and which amounted to a condensed version of a legal education.

Determined to no longer feel victimized and uninformed, I immediately signed up for the program, commuting about 200 miles round-trip for each class. After all the travel and work, I was thrilled when I received the post-graduate certificate in June 1991 which, along with everything I learned, more than satisfied my quest for legal knowledge. Rather than being afraid of the law and tricky lawyers, I now felt like I was part of it. I also felt empowered to utilize the law should it ever become necessary. I remain a firm believer in the power of education as a solution to many of life's most stubborn problems.

What a contrast to when I was a little girl, only two weeks

into the first grade. I still remember sitting on the bench outside the principal's office, determined I would never willingly go back to school. With this constant reluctance, and the belief that I didn't need schooling, I was consistently on the absentee list for several years. However, in high school, I quickly learned there were few jobs available for those without an adequate education. Now, finally, I became a sponge for learning.

Over time, I developed an unquenchable thirst for knowledge. Ultimately, God blessed me with the desire and acuity to become proficient in multiple fields of science as related to personal health. I continued my education in psychology, clinical hypnotherapy, and anesthesiology. I became a licensed naturopath with advanced studies in natural health.

The more I learned, the more I realized how much more there is to learn, and the more I wanted to continue learning.

I became a Master Life Coach. I earned a certification in emotional healing. I became a Board-Certified Expert in Traumatic Stress, a Certified Natural Health Practitioner, and an International Biofeedback Therapist. I even earned a certification in the Quantum Energy Field (QEF).

As a result of all of this training and experience, I was tremendously blessed to receive six lifetime achievement awards in the natural health field. Ultimately, after working closely with several top medical doctors, I was invited to join various medical teams in private practice, including Dr. José Calzada, who told me that he considered me "a fellow colleague." I was having tremendous success helping people overcome their physical and emotional ailments with advanced holistic therapy, and Dr. Calzada, who was aware of my expertise in these areas, wanted me to join his clinic to offer these services to his patients. As honored as I was by his recognition and generous invitation, I felt my purpose was taking me in a different direction.

What I learned, above all, from this period of great learning and growth, was that there is a tremendous amount of wisdom and knowledge out there, well beyond what you find within the confines of each segmented field or discipline. In other words, whether in business, psychology, medicine or law, the experts have only a fraction of all there is to know in their field, and the discipline itself is severely limited by accepted conventions, orthodoxies, and beliefs.

Dr. Joyce with Dr. José Calzada at his office.

I share all of this not to impress you, but to impress upon you that there is hope and possible answers for even the most difficult of life's questions, even when the doctors say that there is nothing else that can be done.

I share this to impress upon you the reality of all of the *unfound* knowledge in the world, and all the *possibilities* that may yet await you, well after you believe, as I did, that your life is nearing its end.

CHAPTER 34

PATHWAYS TO BEING A BETTER MESSENGER

After hearing some great motivational speakers, I wanted to know more about how they developed such wonderful speaking skills. I soon learned they were members of the National Speakers Association (NSA). The NSA has regular meetings and classes, with a local chapter in most large cities.

In order to be a better messenger for God, I joined the NSA in 1987, and quickly found the meetings to be a thrilling change of pace.

I was exceptionally fortunate to get to know personally and learn directly from Cavett Robert, the man who founded the NSA back in 1973. I also met and became well acquainted with Dr. Norman Vincent Peale, the celebrated author of *The Power of Positive Thinking*. Furthermore, I got to know other great legends in the speaking world including Patricia Fripp, Art Berg, Kathy Loveless, and Jeanne Robertson. During this very exciting time, I learned that Australia was even more interested in self-help subjects than the United States. This idea really captured my attention.

I talked with Cavett Robert and Norman Vincent Peale about the possibility and opportunities for the three of us to make a trip to Australia. They thought it was a great idea and plans started falling into place. This is when I first created the expanded version of my *sleep learning* CDs, including *Whispers for Life and Prosperity*, *Whispers for Zest and Cheer for Peace of Mind*, and *Whispers of the Sea of Knowledge*.

However, due to the time-consuming requirements of the lawsuit, it turned out that I was not able to go with them as we had planned.

Over the years, I have often wondered how my life would have been different if I *had* been able to join them on that trip to Australia, helping individuals who wanted to change their lives for the better.

85

Instead, I studied and took courses and became a Naturopathic physician with special training in both traditional and alternative medicine. I have continued to be a learner and healer to this day.

My life was filled with unexpected challenges.

On Father's Day 1998, my husband Earl was experiencing some minor chest pains. We decided to drive to the emergency room to have him checked out. They said that everything was okay, but that they would keep Earl overnight for evaluation. They insisted that I should go home. While driving on the freeway, I felt a soft, but distinct touch on my left shoulder. At the same time, I felt a wave come over my whole being, and I heard Earl's voice telling me that he was on the Other Side. Within less than a minute, I received a call from the hospital telling me to come back. Earl had passed away.

Rather than living only a few weeks, as the doctors said when his heart troubles were first diagnosed in 1984, Earl had lived actively for another 14 years, even with the multiple other serious medical issues he had, ultimately dying of accidental asphyxiation.

As shocked and grief-stricken as I was, I also felt a soft penetrating message from the Lord letting me know that it was Earl's time to come home.

Right after his death, I had an accident and I fell off a step ladder breaking both ankles.

Even though I was deeply grieving and in physical pain, I realized from my near-death experience that I needed to move forward, and make the best use of my own limited Earth time to get God's message out.

CHAPTER 35

RADIO TALK SHOW HOST QUESTION THAT CHANGED MY LIFE

One day in August of 1998, I happened to see a flyer that caught my interest. It was a special class for authors who wanted to be a guest speaker on radio talk shows to share their message.

The flyer seemed to come out of nowhere, and I thought to myself that this is just what I needed. The class was conducted by the renowned former prime-time talk show host, Joel D. Roberts.

Prime-time talk show host Joel D. Roberts.

I knew I needed this class. The class was once a week and was 75 miles away. Even though it was painfully difficult, I made the 150 mile round trip every Saturday for 5 weeks.

There were about 17 people wanting to promote their books in the class, each with various different religious beliefs; including Christian, Christian Scientist, Jewish, but also Atheists and Agnostics.

Knowing of their different beliefs, I felt overwhelmingly intimidated, and was reluctant to speak about my near-death experience and personal message from God.

Joel, the instructor, was sitting at a big round table with a practice microphone (which was not even plugged in). He gave instructions about how to be an interesting guest on a talk show. He even gave tips on how to handle a host when he or she asked questions that might put you in an uncomfortable position. For example, anticipating difficult questions and practicing answering them with confidence.

Knowing the differing beliefs that everyone else in the class had about God, each time my turn came I felt very intimidated and reluctant to speak up to tell my story. The instructor had

87

read my book, knew my story of having died, and was given another chance to live. He knew what I should have been talking about. I was so nervous; I was failing this class big time!

During the last class when it was my turn for the final mock interview, I sat down and felt as if I was on worldwide television. As usual, I was shaking terribly and reluctant to speak.

Joel reached over, took my hand in his, looked me straight in the eyes and said, "Joyce, I want to ask you a question. Do you think God sent you back with a message?"

Boldly and confidently, I replied: "Yes HE did!"

Joel then said firmly, "Do you think your humbleness is getting in the way of God's message?"

I answered adamantly, "Yes it is!" At that moment I felt empowered, determined, and enthusiastic to share God's message with all who would listen about the importance of making it through problems rather than giving up because of them, and how to make certain we enjoy the Other Side when we get there.

Joel then proceeded to interview me as if I were on different types of talk shows that made up for all my previously failed interviews during these classes.

At the end, we each were given a form to write an ad about our books that would be seen by radio talk show producers so they could decide if they wanted to invite us to be on their talk show.

As I was about to leave, Joel gave me the following quote to put on the back of my book: "Dr. Joyce Brown is a hugely inspiring human being… you are bound to be moved by her book and by her."

Also, he said I could be on any talk show in America, and added with a laugh, other than "Howard Stern."

On my drive home from that final class I felt this continued and enlivened passion and purpose to share God's message of the importance of using our limited Earth time wisely to make certain we enjoy the Other Side when we get there. I knew this message would save and change countless lives.

CHAPTER 36

THE HOWARD STERN SHOW

The following week I received my first call from the ad I had previously filled out at the class for authors.

American radio and television personality Howard Stern. Photo: Bill Norton.

When I realized who it was, my eyes popped, my jaw dropped, and my heart began pounding. The man on the phone was a producer, and he invited me to be a guest on Howard Stern's Live Drive-by Show! At the time, Howard Stern's show aired in 60 markets and attracted 20 million listeners.

Even though I was shocked, amazed and apprehensive, knowing millions of listeners heard this show; I controlled my voice and sounded enthusiastic as I bravely accepted.

Immediately afterwards, I began asking other Christian authors if I should go through with this interview. They all told me "yes" and that it may be the only time that Howard Stern's audience might hear my unique message from God.

The producers soon contacted me to make arrangements for our interview to be broadcast live on Howard Stern's coast to coast radio show.

My interviewing skills that I had learned in the class were particularly useful in helping me change his "Howard Stern-type questions" to talk about heaven and the Other Side.

For example, he asked me if they have sex in heaven. I quickly pivoted, and replied, "What I learned on the Other Side was how important it is to use our limited Earth time wisely.

89

And that there are things we can do here while we are still alive to make certain we enjoy Heaven when we get there."

Although it was a great opportunity, it was such a relief when it was over. I was glad that I had this rare and special invitation, and shared my experience and my message with him and his audience.

Over the years, I have to chuckle when people find out and say to me, "*YOU* were on *the Howard Stern Show?*"

CHAPTER 37

STRESS AND GRIEF RELIEF, INC. A LIFE-CHANGING, LIFE-SAVING ORGANIZATION

My passion for saving lives continued to increase. I decided I wanted to form a non-profit organization, and maintain a suicide hotline (877) 375-6923 (877-DR-JOYCE).

With God's help and direction, I met an extremely knowledgeable Enrolled Agent named Jim Quick, who previously helped organize and file multiple non-profits that became some of the top in the nation. Some still feed millions in the world.

In 1999, I founded Stress and Grief Relief, Inc., a 501(c)(3) non-profit organization dedicated to changing and saving lives, preventing suicide and its causes. This is a non-denominational, non-partisan, life-changing and life-saving public charity.

Jim Quick is an amazing, caring, and God-loving man. He helped us fulfill all of the requirements of registering our non-profit with the Internal Revenue Service (IRS), making us eligible for tax-deductible donations, as well as keeping us current with all of the yearly forms and requirements.

Jim has become a dear friend to me. Many of my challenging days have been brightened by Jim's perfectly apt quotes from the Bible.

Even though I believe in God and share my story when I have the opportunity, and when it is appropriate, we work with people from all walks of life, and personal beliefs.

Over the years, I've worked with people of all different faiths. What they all believed in is the importance of using our Earth time wisely and making the best of each day.

Along with a variety of different religious beliefs, and beliefs about God, everyone is at their own individual level of growth. In some places it is not even legal or acceptable to speak about

91

God. As counselors, coaches, and motivational speakers, we work with everyone according to their own specific needs and beliefs.

This book is also about my own life's journey, the promise I made to God about helping others, and my desire to make certain we enjoy the Other Side when we get there.

CHAPTER 38

FALSE PROMISE, REAL FIRE

After we started the non-profit organization, a supposedly honest, religious person arranged for us to receive a donation of a mortgage note on twelve apartments for $250,000. The note was from a third party whose foundation needed to donate to a non-profit in 2001. This would have provided us with an income. After the donation to our non-profit was completed, this individual forged some documents, putting the note and mortgage from the third party in his *own* name so that *he* could collect the rents and live in one of the apartments for free. In essence, he defrauded us of the foundation's note which deprived our non-profit of the income from the apartments.

Over the next few years, we battled in court, which cost high attorney's fees, but we finally won. However, the court costs ate up more than the ultimate recovery. The court finally ruled in our favor in 2006. We technically won, yet somehow, they managed to create more and more horrendous court battles that continued and didn't settle until November of 2019; meanwhile, I still had all of the other stressful situations going on in my life.

Also in 2006, within 24 hours of trying to foreclose on the property with the

Photo of Dr. Joyce's three-alarm house fire which was printed in the local newspaper (you can see the outline of the car rental in front).

twelve apartments that he had taken over, the house I'd previously built and lived in for many years in another state was burned down. Coincidence? The house fire was ruled as set by an unknown arsonist. When the court case was finally settled at the end of 2019, we found out that he had admitted to several people that he did arrange for my house to be set on fire;

however, he died a few years before, and one of his associates was continuing the battle in his name.

Dr. Joyce surveying the damage, searching for any valuables or documents. Sadly, the thieves were almost as bad as the fire.

Dr. Joyce's home before the fire.

CHAPTER 39

GRIEF RELIEF AND A VISIT FROM THE OTHER SIDE

In late June of 2003, I answered the phone and was surprised to hear that my half-sister, Shirley, was found dead. For years, she had been battling depression. Almost monthly, we had discussions by phone, during which I reminded her of reasons she should live. She always seemed to refer to the fact that our father had committed suicide, and that if it was good enough for him (she falsely believed), it was good enough for her.

Shirley's suicide came as a real shock to me, and I felt guilty that I hadn't been able to prevent it. Even though I'd been able to save many other people, I had not been able to save my own sister.

Daily for over a week, I cried and knelt at a particular rocking chair in my living room, asking for Shirley's and God's forgiveness, as I felt I had failed her. One day, as I was kneeling and praying with my head bowed, suddenly, over my left shoulder, I could see her clearly, with an otherworldly vision, even while my head was still bowed and my eyes were closed.

Sharply and firmly, she said, "Joyce, stop! I did this to myself! You always talk about using our time wisely, so stop crying, and grieving so much and move on with your life." Instantly, I felt a peace from God. I knew I was seeing her in a spiritual dimension, and that God and Shirley would work out whatever the consequences of her suicide would be, and that it was not my fault. However, I couldn't stop wondering what exactly Shirley meant when she said she did "this" to herself.

I remember seeing her in such clear and vivid detail. She was wearing a large, white T-shirt that came down past the middle of her thighs. From that moment on, I felt a new feeling of peace and realized that only God knows the intent of the heart, and only God can judge her actions.

About two months after her death, I received a phone call

from a friend of hers who was the executor of her will, and was handling her estate. The woman informed me that my half-sister had left me a small gift.

Before we hung up, I asked her, "What was it with Shirley and a big white T-shirt?"

The lady gasped and said, "That was her favorite T-shirt. She loved that it was so big and comfortable, coming down to almost her knees. She was wearing it the day she died."

This was additional confirmation that God had allowed Shirley to come and tell me not to worry, to lift my grief, and to go on with my earthly life with heavenly peace, and without guilt.

EXPERT TEACHERS, EXCITING TIMES

In July of 2003, I received an unexpected call from my friend Irene Ross, who lived in California. We had both been very active in using and helping others with natural supplements, including those from a leading company with superb products, Nature's Sunshine. Irene invited me to come and stay with her and help with her holistic health clinic.

After a lot of study and work, I had received my license from the U.S. Department of Health and Human Services (HHS) as a qualified Naturopath, and I was looking forward to this new, unexpected opportunity to put this vital knowledge and wisdom into practical use.

Dr. Joyce with Dr. Tennant at one of his specialized training programs.

In addition to helping Irene with her clinic in southern California, I was also excited to have the chance to take additional holistic health classes not available anywhere else.

Previously, I had had such a powerful, transformative learning experience with Dr. Jerry L. Tennant, MD, MD(H), PSc.D, who specializes in a unique healing methodology, that I was eager to discover additional healing modalities. The author of the wildly popular book *Healing is Voltage*, now in its 3rd edition, Dr. Tennant (see picture) continues to serve as an inspiration to me to this day, and I look forward to working with him whenever our schedules allow.

At the time, following my initial training with him, I turned my attention to additional healing methodologies that I could use to complement what I had learned from Dr. Tennant.

Since I was then in California, the next few weeks were jam-packed with special training from top doctors such as Dr. Bernard Jensen, and Dr. David Pesek. Given that I was now much closer to his practice south of the border, I also continued my custom-tailored training with Jose Antonio Calzada, M.D., H.M.D., who is a world renowned expert in stem cell therapy. Dr. Calzada has consulted with the National Olympic Committee regarding infectious diseases, including Zika, and he is an internationally recognized authority in alternative medicine.

Clearly, I was striving to ramp up and augment my knowledge and expertise as a Naturopath around this time, and I was thrilled to be learning from some of the top practitioners in the field. I soon began taking a variety of holistic classes, such as homeopathy, Ayurvedic medicine, enzyme therapy, and other natural health modalities with Melissa Welles-Murphy, another top holistic practitioner with clients and students from all over the world.

While staying in California, I was also doing some limited speaking engagements, and coaching. It seemed like my dreams were coming true, and I felt like I was on top of the world.

CHAPTER 41

A Dramatic, Lasting Change

Along with having learned and gained all this new knowledge and practical experience, 2003 turned out to be quite a year.

It was not only the year of my half-sister's suicide, but there was also a series of unexpected deaths of several close family members and dear friends.

Then, another disaster struck. I had been so busy throughout the holiday season that I had not been able to buy any gifts. So, on Christmas Eve, I decided to drive to the shopping mall. While stopped for the traffic in front of me, I leaned forward to try and see what was holding up traffic.

Suddenly, another car slammed into my van from behind. My head instantly snapped backward, and then forward, as my lower back jerked forward as well.

It turned out to be a three car crash. A crowd gathered around, and someone called an ambulance for me. I was more severely injured than the others. When the paramedics arrived they carefully strapped my head and back to a backboard. They believed my neck and back was broken.

When we arrived at the hospital they took X-rays and CAT scans. Doctors determined I needed to see a specialist not available in that area. With a lot of pain and difficulty, someone provided a ride back to where I was staying with Irene.

I wound up staying with my friend for another year. However, the auto accident crashed my dreams and plans with devastating and lasting physical limitations, and pain. To this day, I am still required to wear a back brace from this accident.

Even with all that I was enduring, I prayed constantly, asking God to help me adapt, and keep my eternal perspective. With determination and prayers, I was able to keep on doing what was essential: helping Irene, dealing with the lawsuits, and doing some coaching.

Before the accident, I had always been extraordinarily

active, doing fun things like line-dancing, the jitterbug, and especially the twist, which I really enjoyed. I could really "cut a rug," let me tell you. Nevertheless, I continued striving to live life to the absolute fullest.

CHAPTER 42

SHARING THE STAGE WITH AN ACTRESS

In May of 2005, I went to a highly recommended health center in California, known for helping cases where others have given up. I had heard great things, and hoped they could help with my pain and inflammation. While I was there, I met a beautiful young woman who had severe stress and depression. During our conversations, I shared my book, told her about my near-death experience, and how important it is for each of us to find and pursue our own purpose for living.

She told me in detail of her definite plan to commit suicide. She felt anger, and held deep grudges against her parents, believing they had not taken proper care of her as a child. She felt her life was hopeless and that her death by suicide would teach them a lesson.

Over the next couple of days, I felt guided to help her understand the heart aches and challenges that her parents and grandparents had in coming from another country, changing cultures, and dealing with extreme financial hardships. I taught her how to meditate, and how to feel calm, serene, and confident. She was also able to increase and improve her memory, which was critical to her work.

She quickly grasped these ideas and feelings and started to change her perspective, and her true, authentic personality burst forth like a blooming flower. With her depression gone, she was now both beautiful inside as well as outside. She was beaming as she told me she was looking forward to finding the right companion, getting married, and having children of her own. She said this would fit perfectly with her career as a movie actress.

She was thrilled with finding her new way of thinking, and her purpose for living. I hadn't recognized her because I rarely go to the movies, but during our conversations I learned others were aware that she was a well-known actress. She invited me to make arrangements to move to Beverly Hills to be her life coach.

101

She reassured me there were others just like her who would like me to be their life coach also. This sounded exciting, and like a perfect fit.

CHAPTER 43

A LIFE CHANGING PHONE CALL

My thoughts of making a new life in Beverly Hills, and of being a mentor and coach for the young actress I'd met at the health resort were suddenly interrupted. I was notified by a staff member that I had an important phone call waiting for me at the front desk of the facility. Once again, my life and plans for the future were, without warning, dramatically changed.

It was from a cousin who explained she had responded to Mother's Life-Alert at 3 a.m., went to her apartment, and found her curled up under the kitchen sink. She was confused and obviously needed hospitalization.

For years, I tried to make sure I called my mom each morning and night to see how she was doing. Then she moved into a senior citizens' facility. Even when I was traveling, I still tried to call her twice a day. I made arrangements for her to wear a Life-Alert device around her neck. I also arranged for family and friends to regularly visit and check on her several days each week.

After I received that surprising phone call about my mother's deteriorating health condition, I knew that my phone calls and others checking on her were no longer adequate. I needed to be there.

My mother could no longer take care of herself. During her three days in the hospital of specialized care for diabetes and dementia, I had arranged for her to go into what I thought was a first-rate care facility where they could eat and socialize together. She was still somewhat independent and believed she was going to be getting married again, even though she was 90 years old. She had heard of rest home romances that had ended in marriage. She thought she might meet someone in this new facility. She was very petite, weighed about 79 pounds, had shrunk to about 4'6," and used a walker. She enjoyed visiting and was outgoing.

With her move to the care facility, I knew that I had to go home to personally make sure how she was doing and wanted to be there with her as much as I could. Though we had not gotten along well and had our challenges, she had given me life and brought me into the world, I knew it was my obligation and privilege to help her with her end of life care.

I had her medical power of attorney. She was on no medications, even for the diabetes. She just required small amounts of food often during the day. I gave explicit written, and witnessed, instructions that she was to receive no medication without my permission.

During this time, I was answering our non-profit suicide hot line, as well as keeping up with doctor's appointments regarding my back injuries. Being a naturopath, I had patients call for advice including one who was in the emergency room who had just had an angiogram and was told he only had two weeks to live. As it turned out, after I worked with him and my doctors team helped him with alternatives to surgery, amazingly, he went on to live a much longer, productive life.

There was a lot going on in my life at the same time as I was taking care of my mother.

Her first couple of weeks seemed to go well. She was outgoing, happy and friendly. She sat in her chair in the doorway of her room and greeted people as they went by. This was in the first part of June. By the end of June, there were dramatic changes. I could tell she had lost weight and she was barely responsive when spoken to.

One morning when I went for my usual daily visit, I found my mother sitting in a little wheelchair in her room, gazing straight ahead. She didn't respond when I talked to her. She had a big, odd-looking bandage on the shin of her little leg. Feeling shocked and surprised, I asked the staff what had happened, but no one had an answer. They just shrugged off my questions and went back to work. I stayed with her until around 9:30 p.m. when I thought she would be safe for the night.

Over the next few days there were additional unexplained injuries and happenings. Even though I arrived by 9:30 a.m. each day, I couldn't imagine what was happening to her when I wasn't there. This was like a living nightmare. I couldn't find any of the staff members who would acknowledge that there was anything wrong.

I realized I needed to get her out of there and into another rest home. Frantically I searched for any information in finding a better place.

A couple of days later, with everything that was going on in my own life, the soonest I could get there was about 9 a.m. When I went into her room this time, I found her lying in bed, clinging to the bed rails, severely shaking with uncontrolled tremors, and she could not communicate with me. I could tell that she could hear me, but just could not respond.

There were state laws that had to be followed in order to transfer her to a different facility. This took about two weeks. It required a lot of hard work to find a better place that met all the state requirements before she could be transferred. I was with her from early morning to late at night.

I didn't know what they were doing, but I knew they were doing something to her. From within my heart and soul, I felt a desire and was compelled to sit in a chair by her bed and sing lullabies for hours. She could not communicate and was now like a little child. But I know she could hear me because unexpectedly, just as I finished one lullaby, she spoke up and said, "I know another one, '*A Little Birdie in a Tree.*'" Those were the last words she ever spoke.

Finally, we had met all the requirements and papers had been filled out; it was time for her to go to the new facility, Hazen Care Center. This new one was a wonderful, loving, caring rest home. The administrator/RN, Romaine Tuft, and her son, Greggory Tuft, arranged to come and get my mother. When they came in the room, Greggory, a husky young man, scooped Mother up, including her bedding. Mom wrapped her arms around his neck as he lifted her up. She was smiling as he carried her. She looked emaciated and I was grateful to get her out of there while she was still alive. We could tell Mother knew she was leaving this place and was very happy about it.

As we were leaving the old facility, the head nurse very begrudgingly gave us my mother's medical records.

What a change the new facility was. Everyone there was happy, well cared for, and seemed to feel contented. However, Mother's condition had deteriorated, and on the third day of our escape, I was so grateful to be sitting by her side when her eyes closed, a tear rolled down her cheek, and she passed to the Other Side.

I felt comforted knowing that when she died, people were around her who sincerely cared. I was so grateful that she did not die alone.

The administrator and head RN of the facility, Romaine Tuft, was so knowledgeable, and caring. She has become a lifelong friend.

During my mother's lifetime, she had helped many family members through their dire circumstances, people who had also lived during the Great Depression and were now already in Heaven. I knew she went home to a place where she had earned her peace of mind and was lovingly greeted by others who were already there. I'm sure they had a grand celebration for having made it through this mortal school of life.

Later, I learned a lot about good nursing homes and bad nursing homes. According to my mother's medical records, she had lost significant weight, down to 64 pounds. Also, contrary to my instructions, I discovered in her medical files from the old nursing home, that they had ordered five shots of Prolixen, a medication for out-of-control schizophrenics. I found out it should not be given to anyone over the age of 65, or under 90 pounds. My mother was 90 years old, and only weighed 64 pounds with her clothes on. My tiny mother was no danger to anyone.

Even though five injections had been ordered, she passed away after the second one. I believe this caused her death. I also found out the potential side-effects of this medication, and similar ones, can be severe shaking, trembling, inability to communicate, and depression. (This is known as Tardive Dyskinesia.)

After finding out about these types of rest homes and their use of medications to control patients, I have helped many others to make wiser choices for the care of their family members.

After her death, I was grieving severely and reminiscing over all the sad parts of my life. I was pleading with God to please help me get over this deep grief and pain and move forward with my life.

CHAPTER 44

MOVING ON

Meanwhile, the phone calls to the suicide hotline continued to come in with people desperately needing help. In time, my prayers were answered, and I was able to move on from the grief and pain of my mother's death.

In the fall of 2005, after having so many disappointments and sadness in my life, one day I received a letter which stated that I was being honored by the Utah Women's Alliance for Building Community. I learned later that I was being honored with the *first* Phyllis LeFevre Lifetime Community Builder Award in recognition of my work with community service programs, police departments, troubled youth, domestic violence, and suicide prevention. They said that my efforts made real and important differences in many communities and people's lives. The award would be presented at a banquet in October. It also invited me to a special luncheon before the event to meet with officers to get to know each other better.

I was surprised and delighted that I had won this prestigious award. I didn't know that anyone was even aware of all the work I was doing.

Later, while I was preparing to attend the banquet, my phone rang from our suicide hot-line. When I answered, I heard a frantic woman's voice say, "I know your organization, Stress and Grief Relief, is known for helping stop suicide. I desperately need your help right now. My brother called me and said that he has his finger on the trigger of his .45 revolver, pointed at his head, and when he pulls it, he will go to instant peace and wanted to tell me goodbye. He said he can't stand the pain after the loss of his wife."

The caller continued telling me she had called the police, who were at his door, but they didn't want to break in because they were concerned he might shoot them or himself. I told her, "Quick, give me his phone number."

This was back when they still had answering machines. I hoped that he might hear me as I was leaving a message. I dialed his number and after three long rings a voice came on that said, "This is John, goodbye to you and goodbye to the world, bury me in peace."

Believing he could hear me over the answering machine, I said, "Don't you want to know where you're going before you pull the trigger on that gun?"

"What if it's worse for you after you die than it is right now? How do I know? I used to be very suicidal. And then I actually died and went to the Other Side."

I kept talking into the recorder, hoping he was listening.

"I found out personally that it's not always nice there regardless of what we have done here on Earth. If suicide is a good idea," I said, "it will still be a good idea next week after you hear my story. Please let me just tell you about it."

Miraculously, what I said piqued his interest. He picked up the phone and gruffly said, "I will hear your story first. But if it's not what you say it is, I'm finishing the job."

He hung up the phone, let the police in, and they took him to a mental hospital.

That same night, I went on to the award ceremony with about 200 guests. I received a fantastic and heart–warming welcome. During my acceptance speech, I had another opportunity to tell my story of having been to the Other Side, discovering my life's purpose, and helping others to uncover their own purpose for living.

I was surprised and excited and felt like I was in another world. It was startling and almost overwhelming, but with their warm encouragement and congratulations, I was able to make a number of new friends.

Early the next morning, I made sure John received my book, *God's Heavenly Answers* at the facility where he'd been taken. In a short time, I found out that he had read my story, requested more books, and started a small suicide prevention group. Soon after he was released, he went back to school, continued his education, and earned his degree in psychology. And he kept on working in suicide prevention. Now John is saving lives.

CHAPTER 45

LIFE IS FILLED WITH SURPRISES

After being a widow for 7 ½ years, a friend arranged a blind date for me with a special man, Ron Runnells, who was retired. This friend believed we had mutual interests.

After dating for a short time, one evening during a candlelight dinner, Ron proposed. It was very romantic and sweet. We felt like we were guided by God to be together at this time in our lives.

He knew about my near-death experience, and he understood and agreed that I needed to continue with my earthly mission. He knew that writing my book, *God's Heavenly Answers*, had been challenging, time consuming, and expensive to publish and distribute to those who needed it, and he understood that I would still keep my author's name, Joyce Hunt Brown.

He also knew I had founded a non-profit organization, Stress and Grief Relief, Inc, and that, along with counseling, a critical part of our strategic vision was (and remains) to get my books and audios out to as many people as we can, helping to prevent suicide and giving hope to the hopeless.

I explained to Ron that we needed to continue to raise funds and receive donations in order to distribute the books and sleep learning recordings in bulk to various groups—including prisons, centers for troubled youth, and individuals, as needed, as well as those who call the suicide hot-line, but also those who have started their own small groups around the book, helping others to overcome depression and find courage, faith, and their own true purpose for living.

After sharing the details around all of the work and expenses involved, I was so excited that Ron was actually looking forward to being a part of our cause, sharing God's message, and our unique coping techniques for stress, depression, grief, anger management, and suicide prevention throughout the world.

We married in January 2006.

My friends got together and gave us an outstanding reception; it was a luau, and included Polynesian entertainers, fire dancers, and fantastic food. Ron has a very special family, that mixed well with my family for this extraordinary occasion. We had two special official witnesses for our marriage ceremony, David W. Allan, the atomic clock scientist for the nation for 32 years, and D.J. Bawden, a well-known famous sculptor for Christian churches all over the world.

Prior to our marriage I knew, Ron, my husband to be, had extensive health problems. The doctors had given him two months to live due to severe heart and kidney problems. They wanted to insert a pacemaker.

However, with years of working with other top health specialists, successfully saving lives, and my own personal experience as a holistic health practitioner, I believed his life could be extended with help from God, holistic care and miracles.

A short time after Ron and I were married, my house was burned to the ground by an arsonist (as mentioned earlier). Ron and I happened to be on a trip in Nevada. This was the house I had built and lived in since 1973. The whole house was engulfed in flames that went over 65 feet in the air. It was what firefighters refer to as a *three-alarm fire*, a serious blaze requiring multiple trucks.

Shock, grief, sorrow and tears—a flood of emotions overwhelmed my entire body. I had just lost everything in my home, including heirlooms, and family keepsakes going back four generations.

In addition, all of my business equipment and records, along with my recording studio, were destroyed. If I had been in my house at the time of the fire, I probably would have died trying to save many of the important records and priceless mementos.

Along with this tragedy, shortly after the house fire, Ron's kidney problems worsened. The neurologist we went to insisted he needed a kidney removed. We made arrangements as soon as possible for his surgery.

After his operation, I discovered the doctor also removed a

healthy adrenal gland in addition to the kidney. When I asked the surgeon why he removed a healthy adrenal gland, I was shocked when he said, "It was faster." He quickly turned, walked away, and began to talk to another patient.

When I had a health issue in the early 1960s, I was given some good advice. I had a good friend who was a general surgeon, and I asked him what I should do. He said, "There are answers, but don't ask a surgeon for a cure for a health issue. Their training and, therefore, their answer will be to have surgery." That certainly applied to Ron's kidney issue, and the removal of his healthy adrenal gland.

After Ron's recovery, I received enough of an insurance settlement from the fire that we went house hunting.

I may have lost my house and everything in it, but the fire insurance money at least opened the way to purchase a new home, replace the furnishings, and at least some of my most important business equipment.

Ron continued to receive specialized holistic health care which really helped his one remaining kidney and prevented him from needing a pacemaker. All of these holistic treatments ended up extending his life from the expected *two months*, given by regular doctors, to the extra *ten years* of living with one kidney.

After we were married, the next ten years of my life was an exceedingly difficult roller coaster. We had some precious good times, and my husband even enjoyed coming with me to some of my holistic health classes, before he had renal failure. Being a caregiver was extremely challenging, but we found ways to keep on keeping on.

In February of 2016, early one morning Ron awoke at about 5 a.m., took my hand in his and said, "I love you, Sweetie," then quietly passed to the Other Side. I became a widow again.

A few days before he passed, we had a talk about the realities of the Other Side, and not being able to communicate with someone, since they can actually hear us, but we can't usually hear them. With a heartfelt plea, I asked him, "If there is any way you can, please let me hear from you when you are on the Other Side."

A while after his passing, I felt prompted to put down some thoughts in the note app on my phone. I wrote, "Many times I'm confined to my reclining power chair. This past year my sweetheart died. Even though I am 83 years old, I am not giving up." Suddenly, a picture of his headstone from the graveyard, appeared between two sentences.

One of the 4 pictures of Dr. Joyce's deceased husband's headstone, which miraculously popped up on her phone.

I went on and finished my notes. About a month later, while I was texting someone, who needed guidance and inspiration, another picture of Ron's gravestone appeared in the middle of the text.

Over the next three months, two more different pictures of his headstone appeared on my phone, for a total of four. I felt a feeling of peace from God for this blessing. I knew that Ron had succeeded in fulfilling my request. This was comforting and helped me face the ordeals ahead.

Over the last two years of Ron's life he required almost constant care. After his passing I grieved extensively and really missed him. I was alone. The house seemed empty. I didn't want to go anywhere or do anything.

Though I was still grieving, I was able to arrange financing to cover the expenses of running the non-profit, including trade show displays, special health care events, key memberships, IANDS events and NSA meetings and workshops.

Life demands that we confront difficult situations. When people call me for grief relief after losing everything in a fire, or any other type of disaster, I am better able to feel empathy and counsel them as they make it through to build a new life.

Sometimes we are to change the situation the best we can. Other times, we must change ourselves.

We all grieve in our own way, even though there are many groups that are adamant that there are specific steps that someone must go through before they feel like going on with life. In my own case, having been a widow twice, and based on my own experience and grief counseling with many others, I know that this is not always true.

To be clear, it is *not* disrespectful to the person we've lost to make the most of our own limited Earth time. Based on my visit to the Other Side, I know that our loved ones would want us to move forward with our lives here on Earth.

What I learned from my near-death experience helped me to move ahead with my life. Whatever Earth time I had left was too short to stay stuck.

In the fall of 2016 and winter of 2017, I participated as a booth exhibitor with our non-profit organization, Stress and Grief Relief, Inc., at several health conferences and conventions. In addition, we had multiple meetings with those interested in near-death experiences and IANDS (International Association of Near-Death Studies).

All of these events required hiring many drivers and others to help me assemble and disassemble the displays. The exhibits proved to be highly effective. Along with other messages, the displays stated that we provide hope to those who feel life is not worth living, and for those who were seeking stress relief now. I was so excited to know that thousands of people were seeing our displays of hope, the importance of using Earth time wisely, and our pioneering ideas about how to learn while you sleep. I was certain the displays and the books that were given out were doing some good.

The meetings and conferences were fun, exciting, interesting, and, as I shared my story, they helped me to become a better messenger, with dramatic, uplifting results.

In part, because I am so eager and determined to spread God's message about how to make certain you enjoy the Other Side when you get there, I carry extra copies of my book wherever I go. It seems I always run into

Dr. Joyce speaking at a Chamber of Commerce meeting.

someone who has a need. Over the years, I've given away countless copies, in addition to those that are donated through our non-profit, Stress and Grief Relief, Inc.

As a result of always having extra copies of my books with me, and giving copies away to those in need, I have heard back from countless people, and learned of a number of interesting and miraculous stories of lives transformed.

CHAPTER 46

FINDING HOPE

My purpose and joy for living is to give hope to others, and an eternal perspective for living. This includes sharing my miraculous recovery from ALS, depression, and wanting to commit suicide, but also overcoming a number of other health crises and heartbreaking setbacks.

Life is filled with challenges and miracles. God is real. We grow and learn from tragedies and problems.

Many people are told their life is ending and nothing more can be done, as I was. Being given a death sentence is not necessarily the full story or the complete truth.

With the help of God, persistence and seeking natural health solutions, many lives are saved.

Because of natural medicine and devoted care giving, my recently deceased husband, Ron Runnells, lived 10 years longer than the doctors' prognosis and my previous husband, Earl Brown, lived 14 years longer than the doctors expected.

CHAPTER 47

LIVING A LIFE WITH CHALLENGES, WHILE STILL SHARING HOPE

Now at almost 90 years old, I am able to continue enjoying a busy lifestyle as I share what I learned while I was in Heaven during my near-death experience, and unique techniques for overcoming depression, anger, stress, and changing and saving lives.

Additionally, I feel driven to do all I can, while I can, which includes fulfilling speaking requests and interviews, conducting personal and group consultations, and continuing to write more books. Whenever and wherever possible, and appropriate, I share God's message of using our Earth time wisely.

Unfortunately, I still experience severe back pain from the auto accidents and failed back surgeries. In the summer of 2017, my doctor ordered multiple MRIs of my entire neck and back.

Dr. Joyce at her Stress and Grief Relief booth before one of the numerous trade shows.

Five compression fractures in my vertebrae were discovered. Additional areas of pressure on the spinal cord were also found, as well as three more herniated disks. These were new complications in the situation with my spine. The doctors were stunned and said that I could end up paralyzed or die at any time. By continuing to "keep on keeping on," I'm surprising them all.

Due to this condition, I can only walk short distances, and sit up for a limited time each day. This may slow me down, but it does not stop me. There are times when I need my reclining power chair in order to lie back. Then, whenever I need to go from place to place, I return it to its full upright position, or I jump on my Harley mobile. Regardless of how I move around, the fact is that most others still have trouble keeping up with me.

To be clear, despite the other challenges I have to navigate, I have not had any more symptoms of ALS since I was healed in 1988.

I do not dwell on what I cannot do. Instead, I feel forever grateful for the opportunities I have, and for new chances to learn and be of service.

After many years of continued challenges and calamities in my life, in February of 2017, I finally found the time to rejoin the Las Vegas chapter of the National Speakers Association.

Dr. Joyce returning from an afternoon ride on her Harley mobile.

NSA Las Vegas has outstanding meetings, with training and coaching from remarkable speakers, including four International Toastmasters Champions—Mark Brown (1995), Craig Valentine (1999), Ed Tate (2000), and Darren LaCroix (2001)—as well as outstanding guest speakers from other chapters across the nation, such as Patricia Fripp, Michael Hauge, Ford Saekes, and

Dan Clark. They all share their unique, motivational, life changing techniques.

I found it enlightening to hear about their particular methods of speaking to their audiences. This is helpful when I tell my story and the lessons I've learned. Since I've been applying what they taught, while being a part of the NSA group, not only am I reaching larger audiences, but more of my listeners are letting me know that they feel inspired and closer to God, and are coming up with good reasons to make it through their problems.

Each speaker has their own style for motivation with the end goal being to help each individual in their audience to find and improve their own lives.

At NSA they share their special methods with us, their fellow speakers. At every meeting there is always a new tip and information that I can apply to the way I share my story.

I've enjoyed mingling and getting to know a number of these people better. I love listening and learning from their stories and outstanding presentations. Several of these extraordinary people have become like family to me.

CHAPTER 48

NEVER GIVE UP

Even though only God can ultimately judge someone's actions, my visit to the Other Side showed me just how important it is to not give up on life, but also for each of us to find our own true purpose for living. This can bring feelings of zest and joy. It also helps in overcoming problems and attaining peace of mind for ourselves and others. As we live our purpose optimistically, with prayer, courage, and faith, rather than giving up, we are more apt to receive miracles, and enjoy the Other Side when we get there. Using the power of "positive belief," we can change our self-talk which can change our lives.

I know there are some people who say it does not matter how we live our lives, or how we use our Earth time. However, what if it does make a difference? Remember what the Bible says: "Do unto others as you would have them do unto you." Also, "Love thy neighbor as thyself." Putting these simple truths into practice will bless many lives and can create miracles for ourselves and others.

My personal experience dispels the myth that just by dying you can automatically receive peace of mind, regardless of how you've lived your life.

Our time here on Earth is too valuable to waste. I am grateful for what I can still do and accomplish each day. Prayer, wisdom, and inspiration help guide us through our lives. What a difference the world would be if we could all be more Christ-like.

Over the years, I have had a wide variety of opportunities to share God's message and His heavenly answers for us all. When people tell me their success stories, it touches my heart, and they become my mental cheerleaders. I feel energized with joy and peace in my soul as I continue trying to fulfill my purpose for living as I promised God I would do.

CHAPTER 49

MY JOURNEY THROUGH BLINDNESS

In November of 2011, even though I had been getting injections in my eyes since 2009, my vision was totally lost. It was so far gone, in fact, that I needed a flashlight to see a glass of water at my side. I was told by eye specialists that I had both dry and extreme wet macular degeneration and that my vision would never get better since it had suddenly gotten so much worse, even after all the injections.

Normal vision is 20/20, but legally blind is 20/200. When asked to read the eye chart, I couldn't even see the chart. The assistant pulled up a chair in front of me. She held up her fingers and said to tell her when I could see them. I couldn't see anything until her fingers were below her shoulders. Then I could barely make out two fingers in my peripheral vision. I asked her if anyone had ever gotten their vision back when it had progressed to this point.

She answered, "I'm sorry, no."

I said with faith, "Then, I will be the first."

Dr. Joyce with Bill Sardi, "The Vitamin Supplement Answer Man."

At the time, I'd had injections in each eye to supposedly slow down the bleeding in both retinas. Unfortunately, after over 70 injections it still had not worked.

I had heard resveratrol could help with vision. I had also previously taken eight different supplements with various brands of resveratrol, but was disappointed that none of them made any difference.

In 2012, I was introduced to Bill Sardi, an expert in all aspects of improving vision, health, nutrition and living a longer healthier life. Known as the "Vitamin Supplement Answer Man," Bill had the perfect solution for my problem, an effective natural supplement, Longevinex, which includes a special formula and type of resveratrol. He sent it to me overnight.

Surprisingly, after taking it for just a few days, my vision was miraculously restored to the point I could thread a needle. I was also able to renew my driver's license.

Shortly thereafter, the story of my vision being restored was covered in-depth by the Emmy and Peabody award-winning journalist George Knapp on CBS News.

In June 2013, the National Academy of Television Arts and Sciences awarded George Knapp and KLAS with an Emmy for their story about my restored vision using Longevinex, entitled *Miracle Eye Cure.*

However, even though my vision restoration was miraculous, however, the number of injections was misstated as only being 17, when it actually had been over 70, which was even more miraculous. But it was too late to fix it after the story was published and distributed.

I was excited when Bill Sardi invited me to a luncheon in Las Vegas to meet Dr. Stuart Richer O.D., Ph.D., President of the Ocular Nutrition Society. I learned that Dr. Richer had been working with multiple patients who had macular degeneration who got their vision back after taking Longevinex®.

In fact, referring to Longevinex, Dr. Richer writes, "Macular degeneration affects millions of senior adults. There is no proven remedy for this insidious sight-robbing disease. The fact that a nutraceutical (Longevinex®) has been demonstrated for the first time to reverse a predictive measure for macular degeneration is a monumental development in preventive medicine."

Unfortunately, over a few years, I developed some new and very serious vision problems because of scarring from the previous extensive bleeding in my retinas, prior to taking the resveratrol supplement.

As bad as my vision problem is today, it is still not nearly as bad as when my vision was totally *gone* because of severe wet macular degeneration. If only I had known about and taken Longevinex earlier, I know I would not have had any macular degeneration in the first place.

It's my belief anyone over the age of 60 should take Longevinex® as a needed health supplement to prevent age related macular degeneration. I strongly suggest you call the Longevinex® office, ask for information about the product and request their newsletter which has tremendously helpful health information not found anywhere else. Bill Sardi personally writes the newsletter. It's exceptionally informative and helps us understand how to improve our health at the cellular and even molecular level.

There was another episode in my life that convinced me of the importance of continuing to take Longevinex. During my doctor's visits in 2017, when I was told I could become paralyzed or die at any time because of the severe pressure on my spine, I felt shocked. When I came home, I was still in shock. There were other things in my life that took priority with my limited time, and I overlooked taking any of my supplements. I began to concentrate on other things that seemed to be more important.

However, about a month before, since it had been nearly three years since I had my eyes checked, I had made a new appointment. This was after receiving the bad news from the previous doctor, who had given me the shocking news about my spinal condition.

When I went to the eye specialist, and while they were examining deep inside my eyes with their special equipment, the doctor said, "Oh, your left eye is hemorrhaging in the retina."

As he said that, I realized I'd forgotten to take my Longevinex® during the past few weeks. I spoke up quickly and asked for another appointment for him to check it again in two weeks. After I arrived home, I immediately got back on my daily resveratrol regimen.

Two weeks later, when I returned for my appointment and

the doctor rechecked my eyes, he was surprised and said, "The hemorrhaging has stopped."

With a sound of utter disbelief, he repeated, "There is no more bleeding in your retina."

I could tell he was astonished. He seemed very perplexed, but he did not ask why. I tried to tell him about Longevinex, but he was too busy to listen.

This experience reinforced my determination to take the resveratrol supplement *every day*. I also take it because I've had heart problems for years. I've read scientific studies on animals which demonstrate that Longevinex can reduce the size of a heart attack (as measured by scar tissue), reduce the death of heart muscle cells, double the heart pumping pressure, and increase the blood flow in the aorta (*Health Freedom News*, Winter 2017).

Back in 2012, I had my husband Ron start taking Longevinex for his slow and irregular heartbeat (atrial fibrillation, often referred to as "A-Fib"), which, at the time, he had had for more than 25 years. The body is electrical, and when it gets out of balance it can cause health problems such as irregular heartbeat. As a result of Bill Sardi's recommendation, Ron took Longevinex, water-soluble B1, and Magnesium. He did not need a pacemaker as his physicians had previously proposed. Not only did the A-Fib completely disappear, but it also significantly improved his heart condition, and even improved his vision.

Dr. Nathaniel Lebowitz, a physician specializing in preventive cardiology, also stands behind resveratrol and this particular resveratrol supplement. In fact, he has stated, "A particular brand of resveratrol, Longevinex, is recommended to our patients because it is the only brand that has been shown to reduce damage to the heart better than plain resveratrol in experimental animal studies. I've been recommending a resveratrol pill for my patients for over a decade now. Among all the medicines I use," Lebowitz continues, "this dietary supplement is the one that has the most promising science behind it."

I am also aware of studies that have shown Longevinex has an anti-aging benefit, enabling people to live longer, healthier lives.

Even though I have some vision problems now, it is much better than the total vision loss I had in November 2011. With the continued use of resveratrol, it has stopped the bleeding for over eight years. I've not required any more injections since then, even though the doctors previously told me I would have to have them for the rest of my life.

The low vision I have now is caused by the *scarring* from the previous bleeding from years ago. Had I known years ago what I know now, I believe these vision problems could have been prevented.

I am aware of and have personally tried thousands of dollars of low vision products, most of which did not work for me, but may work for others, and still additional products which are just false promises or scams.

I know of numerous other people who have had miraculous results with their vision using this particular product. I faithfully use Longevinex, and regularly recommend it, but I do not sell it. Of course I cannot promise what it will do for others, but it's worked wonders for me and many others I know personally. I believe it is only available directly from the company. For more information, visit Longevinex.com.

As I often share whenever I conduct health workshops, host a booth at a health fair, or do health counseling, as much as

I can I share info about Longevinex®. In fact, as a bonus, I hold drawings for free boxes of Longevinex®. As I often say, Bill Sardi has the story about "how" to live longer, and I have the story about "why" to live longer.

This has been another part of my life's journey of finding hope and miracles which I often share with those who are having vision problems.

CHAPTER 50

FINDING PEACE OF MIND

My soul still yearns to share with family, friends, and the whole world, regarding the importance of making it *through life's problems*, rather than quitting life because of them. Whenever and wherever possible, I have related my personal story and the potential eternal benefits or consequences of utilizing our Earth time wisely.

I feel heartfelt gratitude that numerous people have responded to my message. I have received miraculous accounts and priceless personal stories.

Many, including their family members, have expressed gratitude for receiving a new Other Side perspective for living. They are now helping to share God's message, to "keep on keeping on," despite the countless challenges they face here on Earth.

The good news is, with God's grace and in His timing, survivors of those who have lost a loved one *can* find peace and comfort to continue their own individual life's journey.

I feel immense joy when I hear back from others who have overcome their negative attitudes, feel better about the life they're now living, hope to have a more pleasing life review when they are on the Other Side, and feel better prepared to meet God when their time comes.

The following are just a handful of examples of the type of responses I have received. Perhaps you may know someone who is struggling with similar problems and may benefit by learning eternal truths, and from other's success stories.

"Dr. Joyce Brown had given me a copy of her book (*God's Heavenly Answers*). I was going through a lot at that time and was addicted to drugs. I started reading the book but ended up in jail before I could finish it. Joyce visited me in jail and arranged for me to get another copy of her book so I could finish it, which I did while I was in custody. I can't tell you the power that book had on my life. I'm now

128

16 months clean. Some days are really rough, but I make it through the day with the hope Joyce shares in her book. It had a life-changing effect on me. I just want to thank you, Joyce, for having the courage to write this book. It has helped me immensely. I will always have a special place in my heart for you."

—Barbara Cimino, former drug addict.

"After hearing the details of your Other Side experience, I have found reasons why I want to live instead of constantly wishing I could die or wanting to trade places with someone else."

—Michelle L., Student, age 14

"Dear Joyce, Thank you for writing your book. I read and re-read it often in order to convince myself that life is worth living, no matter how painful or difficult it gets. I have many extremely difficult health problems. In fact, I have been to the Other Side myself. I had become too 'heavenly minded to be any earthly good' by wanting to be there instead of here. After a series of tragedies causing me to lose almost everything, I didn't want to live anymore. Your book has helped me dramatically. It is such a strong and effective tool against suicide that I wrote letters and sent books to relatives, friends and loved ones. I hope and pray your message will be spread by radio and TV interviews and even a movie. Best wishes and thanks with all my heart."

—Sheila Wall.

"I will forever be grateful to Dr. Joyce for saving my youngest daughter's life. When she found evidence that suggested her husband was cheating on her, she overdosed on meds and attempted to take her life. After hours in a coma, the medical personnel were able to bring her around. She was devastated that her suicide attempt had failed and was absolutely determined to try again, someplace where she wouldn't be found in time.

"Feeling helpless, I brought her to my home and gave her Dr, Joyce's book, *God's Heavenly Answers* to read. While I didn't expect her to, she did, indeed read it, and her whole attitude changed. She was able to call Joyce, who was willing to have long conversations with her. She had a small son at the time who really needed his mommy, so what a blessing it was to her loved ones that she was willing to read that book and accept help!

"Now, several years later, she is a happy homemaker, stressed with medical problems like MS, but determined to hang in there and make the most of what she has been dealt. So, thank you with all my heart, Dr. Joyce Brown!"

"PS: I never did learn if her husband really was unfaithful, but he's very devoted to her since."

—Lily Palmer

"A friend gave me Dr. Joyce Brown's book. To pacify her, I agreed to read a few pages, although I had definitely decided to commit suicide that day—my suicide note was already written. But I couldn't put the book down. I then saw my world from a new perspective and wanted to share this life-changing, life-saving, near-death account with loved ones and friends. The next day I ordered 20 books to give out to friends and family."

—Helen Johnson

"This book is a self-contained support system."
—Karen Anderson

These are just samples of the many letters I have received letting me know of the countless lives that were changed after hearing and applying God's messages.

We all make mistakes in our lives. However, even if someone's yesterdays are scarlet, with God's help their tomorrows can be snow white.

It is my hope and prayer that by telling my life story, including eternal truths, it will cause a ripple effect throughout the world for many generations to come.

It is important that we use our Earth time wisely. There *is* life after life. We *can* make certain we enjoy the Other Side when we get there.

As author and composer Janice Kapp Perry said about *God's Heavenly Answers*, "The day after I read this book, I viewed my life from a completely different, and much improved perspective. It's great to be reminded in such a compelling way about what matters most—now and in eternity."

Prolific American composer, songwriter, and author Janice Kapp Perry.

CHAPTER 51

BELIEVE IN MIRACLES

Many times, people ask me, "Why have you had so many problems?" I always tell them, "We develop physical muscles by lifting weights. We develop mental and spiritual muscles by overcoming problems or making it through setbacks and challenges without giving up."

It may not have seemed like it at the time, but by making it through problems, they became opportunities for me to learn and grow. As I made it through challenges, each of them helped me develop empathy, and gain the ability to better help others going through similar situations. Ultimately, the difficulties became a blessing in disguise.

With sincere prayers, I want to be a true messenger, and keep sharing God's eternal truths. Life is too short to be easily offended, angry, have self-defeating thoughts, or hold grudges.

As I said before, it is important to become Christ-like, loving, kind, forgiving and merciful, *especially while driving*.

Since I am in my ninth decade and do not know how much more time God will grant me, I am having a bench made for my grave with my message to the world:

Our Lord God Is Real!

Now is not forever. Life is a journey, not a destination,

Love life and others.

Remember: We can create miracles for ourselves. If you have been diagnosed with ALS, or any other illness, and the doctor says, "nothing more can be done," keep searching for physical, mental, and spiritual solutions until you find what works for you.

One of my favorite sayings is:

Believe in Miracles,

Expect Miracles,

Be a Miracle for someone else.

CHAPTER 52

Looking Back on My Life's Journey

In my struggles for health, to live, to walk, to see, to succeed, I have had to overcome what seemed impossible obstacles by worldly standards. With the help of God, I have endeavored to painstakingly build the obstacles into heavenly stepping-stones of understanding more thoroughly what this life is all about. I am trying to fulfill my real purpose in life, caring and sharing.

As I look back now, I realize gratefully, with God's help, I made it through so many different trials and tribulations throughout my life, including ALS, depression, terrible auto accidents, the death and loss of loved ones, a devastating house fire at the hand of a bitter arsonist, my own struggles with thoughts of suicide, and the loss of my father, half-sister, and four cousins to suicide.

I can now see that as I searched and pleaded for solutions to my problems, I gained knowledge, wisdom, and information that can truly help me and many other people.

In fact, going through these many things led me to create our non-profit organization, Stress and Grief Relief, Inc. A vital part of this is work is helping those struggling with the loss of a loved one—particularly those who are grieving after the suicide of a family member or friend—so they can find hope, Heavenly peace of mind, and move forward with their own lives. I truly understand how they feel.

Death is not the end. There is life after life. Again, it is so important to understand that your loved ones, when they die, they become your spiritual cheerleaders and want you to make the most of whatever Earth time you have left. None of us know for sure if we have a tomorrow.

I also learned our pets go to heaven, receive peace and joy, and we will see them again. (More information about animals going to heaven and being able to communicate is in my companion book, *God's Heavenly Answers*.) Having just recently lost my constant 9-year-companion, Kitty, this is a subject close to my heart. In fact, I have begun writing a new book entitled, *The Secret Life of My Little Service Dog Named Kitty and Proof She Went to Heaven.*

I also reaped countless miracles. At almost 90 years old, I am truly a transformed person.

We are here to "learn the lessons of life." The wisdom I've acquired while going through trials, challenges and calamities have cost me dearly. My soul's sincere desire is to share with all who want to improve their own mental and spiritual well-being. We need to care for our lives, we need to care for our planet. There are ways and means to attain a better quality of living with courage, faith and hope.

My quest for answers has taken me to the far corners of the world. I have been privileged to visit the legendary "Holy Mountains" and even the mysterious "Lost Caves." Miraculously, I was given the opportunity to work with top scientists, world-recognized engineers, and internationally acclaimed physicians. I have researched and explored both modern and ancient manuscripts and have discovered some of the greatest eternal truths of the ages.

Yes, my life has been blessed with miracles, but I had to *reap* them. Over the last 80-plus years, my life has been a miraculous journey. I enjoy teaching others how to reap miracles too!

Each of us can be more, have more, and do more for ourselves, and others, and for this world. We can have a happier life, and a cleaner environment. We can grow rich mentally and spiritually. We can have more time for fun, profit, and for reaping miraculous results.

American clergyman Edward Everett Hale wrote in *The Power of One*, "I am only one, but still, I am one. I cannot do everything, but still, I can do something. And because I cannot do everything, I will not refuse to do the something that I can do." As I share my message with those who want to listen, I believe we can all do something to help make this world a better place. Whatever we can do, with the help of God, if we *will* do it, we can make this a better world for us all.

What I sincerely desire is success—not success the way the world defines it, but success the way Ralph Waldo Emerson defined it in his 1909 essay, *Success*:

"To laugh often and much;

To win the respect of intelligent people and the affection of children;

To learn the appreciation of honest critics and endure the betrayal of false friends;

To appreciate beauty,

To find the best in others;

To leave the world a bit better, whether by a healthy child, a garden patch or a redeemed social condition;

To know even one life has breathed easier because you have lived.

This is to have succeeded."

CHAPTER 53

APPLYING THE PRINCIPLES: STORIES FROM CONQUERING HEROES IN THE BATTLES OF LIFE

The following are stories from a few special friends, some of whom are also members of the National Speakers Association (NSA). These particular friends have read my book, know my story, and are sharing with their audiences the wisdom of living life to the fullest, rather than being stuck feeling overwhelmed with challenges and stress. I thought you would find their stories to be both inspirational and powerful examples of how others have applied the Heavenly wisdom and principles shared throughout this book. Their messages were written and shared especially for this book, to help you with your own journey through life.

Judi Moreo: You Name It

International Speaker, Author, and Coach

Judi and I first met at a National Speakers Association (NSA) chapter meeting in Las Vegas. We hit it off right away, and have become dear friends ever since. I greatly respect and admire her as a person. In fact, Judi is a great inspiration and example to me personally, and I believe she would be an exceptional role model for you as well. What I admire most about Judi is her persistence and intelligence and how she always has so much knowledge to share. I also love how she is able to make people feel comfortable, and how she shares what she knows in a way that hits home.

After speaking in major cities across the globe, and authoring nearly a dozen books, including two international bestsellers—*You Are More than Enough* and *Conquer the Brain Drain*—Judi is now one of the most recognized personal growth trainers and coaches in the world.

She started her first business with a mere $2,000, but a lot of chutzpah, and now, decades later, enjoys a devoted following of clients and fans around the world. She has spoken in twenty-nine countries, and has received numerous awards, including the prestigious Certified Speaking Professional designation from the National Speakers Association, which puts her in the top tier of international speakers.

Looking back to her personal experience conquering cancer, the following is the message that she wanted to share with my readers:

Judi Moreo: There are two types of stress: distress, which is the tough kind and can also make us sick, and eustress, the good kind, that helps us have extraordinary strength. So how do we know which is good and which is bad? As they would say where I grew up in South Texas, "It ain't nothin' til I say what it is." Therefore, when things get tough or tense, I have a tendency to say it is the good kind of stress. My parents taught me to always look for the good in any situation.

So, while experiencing cancer was a shock, at the same time, it was a good kind of stress. I came to a very clear understanding of what is really important in my life. I learned to be more tolerant and a bit more compassionate. I learned to be less judgmental and more accepting. Most of all, I learned to be more grateful for every day and every breath.

I learned not to let people, no matter how expert, rush me into making decisions, to eat only foods that will nourish my body and give me energy, to stop when I'm tired and rest, to spend time with people I love and stay away from those who add nothing positive to the quality of the moments in my life. I learned to do things, go places, and be with people because it's what I want. Most of all, I learned to trust God 100%.

In life, we either have fear or we have faith. I see distress as a form of fear. Therefore, there is no room for it in my life. My faith has pushed it out.

We make many choices every day. When we choose to trust God, take part in creating our own destiny, show gratitude for the progress we've already made and stay focused forward, we see miracles at every turn. There just "ain't no room for unhealthy stress."

Mr. Kim Cherry: The Power of Positive Belief

Businessman, Entrepreneur, Engineer, and Inventor

Kim and his wife, Kay, and I first met at my home in 2017 when they traveled all the way down from Idaho to visit. They were with Patricia Tamowski and Scott Douglas who were deep in their research and documentary work around ALS reversals (see Chapter 30).

Kim had been diagnosed with ALS several years earlier, and when they learned from Patricia and Scott that I had reversed ALS in 1988, we all agreed to get together to help further the work of learning about ALS and how others may be able to reverse it as well.

From the moment we first met, I knew that Kim and Kay are very special people. They just radiate hope and helpfulness, and I always feel better just by being around them. They seem to have this positive energy that is almost electric. But what really stands out about Kim and Kay is the way they seem to be tuned in to the needs and concerns of others.

They remind me of topics I often speak about: the importance of positive thinking and positive belief, and how we have to believe in miracles and expect miracles if we hope to reap miracles, but also how we should look for ways to be a miracle for someone else.

I will always remember the time soon after we met, that I was stranded at home unable to get a ride to an important meeting (as you may recall, due to the scarring in my retinas, I am unable to drive). Suddenly, out of nowhere, Kay calls me and says, "Hi, Joyce. I just wanted to call and see if you needed anything. I was just thinking of you, and wondering if there might be something I could do for you." My mouth hung open for a moment; I was blown away. I told her about the meeting, and how I desperately needed a ride, but was unable to find one. Kay immediately agreed to get me to the meeting. Of course it was a terrifically kind gesture, but what really surprised me was how she seemed to know that I was in need at that exact moment. It was a miracle.

As you'll read below, Kim has an amazing story about his experience with ALS. He also has a number of vital lessons to share. One of the things that really stands out to me about his story is how dedicated both he and Kay were to reversing Kim's ALS, and the in-depth approach they were willing to develop to help ensure their success.

As you may have already picked up by now, and will continue to learn as you continue reading the stories below, people conquer ALS, MS, Parkinson's, Alzheimer's, and so many other dreaded, deadly diseases, along with depression, divorce, grief, and any number of other grave life challenges, with a range of different methods or game plans. And while there are certainly a number of critical commonalities (e.g. prayer, maintaining a positive attitude, having a clear purpose, etc.), some people find success with just a few specific practices, or particular changes (e.g. removing their silver amalgam fillings). Others make a great many changes, yet still end up with the same, or a very similar result. Likewise, while some find they are healed rather quickly, others may take many years before they reach their goal.

As you will see in his story below, Kim has been willing to make a great many changes to virtually every aspect of his life. What we can all learn from both him and Kay is the importance of continuing to seek God, and, no matter how trying your circumstances in the moment, the importance of never giving up. We cannot know God's ultimate plan, but we can choose to do all we can. And Mr. Kim and Kay Cherry are outstanding examples of this principle in action.

Mr. Kim N. Cherry: I was 63 years old when I was diagnosed with ALS on November 22, 2011. This was after some 16 months of tests and misdiagnoses leading to an open-heart surgery and unproductive treatments for asthma, emphysema, and COPD. My condition was advanced. I was told that my ALS was fatal, unstoppable, and untreatable. I was told that the normal survival time for PALS (Persons with ALS) is three to five years from diagnosis. In a visit with my primary care physician just a few days later, I was told I had a year, and that I would never see two. I was diagnosed with both Lower Motor Neuron and Upper Motor Neuron, or Bulbar ALS.

I am a successful businessman, entrepreneur, engineer, and an inventor. To hear such declarations from doctors that I had come to trust was disheartening at best, and contrary to my whole life's approach to obstacles. After a few days of serious contemplation from the original diagnosis, my wife (Kay) and I made the decision that we would not accept the prognosis and that we would do all in our power to fight this disease. The doctors discouraged us from seeking any alternative therapies, saying they would only take our money and give us false hope. Though they said there was nothing more they could do, this did not mean there was nothing we could do. False hope is better than no hope.

I refused the only FDA approved drug for ALS, Riluzole/Rilutek and the "opportunity" to attend an ALS clinic. I felt the ALS clinics are there to measure decline, offer the next prop to the grave, and give you no hope to heal.

By mid-January 2012, we decided to end our association with everyone, friend or professional, that was not positive and did not believe we could beat this disease. The power of the mind is a huge part of healing any disease. My traditional doctors refused to see any benefit from our initial holistic steps.

In early December 2011, shortly after receiving the diagnosis, we went to a chiropractor, Dr. Jared Nielsen, in Heber City, Utah, about 300 miles from our Idaho home. He did some testing and said I had mercury poisoning, fungus, and gluten sensitivity. There went the homemade bread. I started the supplements he recommended to help with glutathione production and fungus reduction.

Faith in God, special religious blessings, and the love and prayers of friends and family, as well as our own prayers have played a huge part in my success. I believe God helps those who work to help themselves. Through our internet research (which Kay heads, and continues yet today) and tips from family and friends, we found things that have worked for us.

I recognize that this insidious disease is different for most everyone that falls under its curse. The primary challenges I faced were my ability to breathe, and my ability to swallow—both Bulbar issues. I simply could not get enough oxygen and felt I was slowly suffocating most of the time, but especially at night when lying down, sometimes taking 20 to 30 minutes to work my way down from a propped up sitting position. I was choking on liquids, and even on my own saliva. My lungs were filling with fluid. My right calf had atrophied considerably, and I had lost most of the strength in my right leg. And my hands and forearms were rapidly declining. I had severe drop foot, and my ankles would turn at the slightest misstep. Though I could still walk, my balance was shot. I was losing my ability to speak. I felt I simply could not get enough air to make the words come out. Walking more than a couple dozen steps required a breather, and a simple flight of stairs was daunting, requiring a mid-climb rest and a couple minutes recovery at the top. Also, the cold air seemed to almost shut my breathing functions down. I was experiencing severe muscle cramps, especially in my feet, calves, and thighs, sometimes experiencing two or three cramps at the same time.

We started with Dr. Nielsen's program immediately. Things did not get immediately better. About the middle of January, I survived a couple of the worst nights of my life, sitting up all night on a sofa, fighting for every breath. It was then that I started using supplemental oxygen, which really helped.

By late January, we started seeing improvement in my ability to breathe, though fatigue and strength were still serious issues, as was the cold. But perhaps one of the biggest benefits of meeting with Dr. Nielsen, is that he was the first professional that told me I had a good chance to beat the disease. Not only did I believe him, but I believed that he believed it too.

In April of 2012, we added ozone and hyperbaric [oxygen therapy] to our protocol. The treatments with the ozone and hyperbarics originally took from 4 to 6 hours a day. I gave myself an ozone IV three times a week for the first two months, then cut back to two times a week through most of 2012. I had an IV port placed in the summer of 2013, which greatly simplified my IV treatments.

I mentioned earlier that my improvement has been phenomenal. I started playing golf again, riding a cart, in March of 2012 (see photo). We sold our primary business in June 2012.

We spent the winter of 2012-2013 seeking warm weather and lower elevation to help with my breathing issues. When we returned from Texas in the spring of 2013, l knew that I had made great progress.

In the summer of 2013, I had my mercury fillings replaced by biologically safe methods. Also in the summer of 2013, we decided we could not just stand by and let others suffer if what we had learned was helpful. Kay began a website in 2013 and continues adding to it monthly. You may reach us through ALSWinners.com should you like to contact us.

I continued to have hand and leg cramps periodically, up until November or December of 2012, but now seldom have any, even after walking a round of golf, as long as I make sure I stay well hydrated. I was also able to start swimming again. Staying hydrated at the beginning was difficult as fluid was going into my lungs with every swallow. Drinking carbonated water stimulated throat muscles to help with that problem. In 3 years, that throat muscle completely healed.

The supplements we felt were the most important are magnesium for muscle issues, alpha lipoic acid for toxins and free radicals, lion's mane mushroom to rebuild myelin sheath around the nerves, astaxanthin for free radical damage and oxidative stress, turmeric with black pepper for inflammation, CoQ10, Vitamin D3, and Vitamin B12. We also used Essential oils to help heal the spine, and Breathe, another essential oil to help my breathing. Using a magnesium rub or magnesium lotion can help those occasional muscle cramps.

Food changes included going gluten free, eliminating sugars, and changing the oils we used. Coconut oil is the best for PALS. We eat mostly organic foods and meats grown without antibiotics and hormones. We got rid of cleaning chemicals in the home and found "clean" sources. We changed the personal care products which are loaded with bad chemicals. We suggest PALS get rid of soda pop, alcohol, tobacco, and other unhealthy products including all fast foods. I had become and continue to be very sensitive to tobacco smoke, perfumes, colognes, and other similar products as they shut my lungs down. However, the smells of the natural essential oils never bothered me.

My progress on my reversal continued slowly for the first 6 years, but I had a major setback in early 2018, due to an infection of my IV port. This resulted in two hospital stays, the first for two weeks in St George, Utah in February and the second for ten weeks from mid-May through July in Idaho, a battle with sepsis, two mini strokes, and a second open-heart surgery. The biggest carry over from this setback is constant vertigo, which has greatly affected my golf game and ended my swimming and bike riding. Though I still have some ALS symptoms, particularly with my gait and balance, and of late with my breathing, I expect to continue to heal. I may never be completely free of the disease, but I can LIVE with what I have.

Best wishes and God's speed to all PALS,

Mr. Kim N. Cherry

Stormie Andrews: Listen to Understand

Author, Speaker & Co-Founder of Yokel Local

Stormie Andrews and I first met at a National Speakers Association chapter meeting in Las Vegas. We have been fast friends ever since. What I admire most about Stormie is his

commitment to excellence and service. Stormie has had remarkable success in multiple different performance-based industries. Whenever someone asks him about his success, one of the themes that comes up again and again is his commitment to providing significantly more value to his clients and customers than anyone else in the field. When I invited Stormie to contribute to this book, he immediately began thinking of what he could say to provide as much value as possible. That's when it hit him. He recently learned one of the most difficult, heart-wrenching lessons of his life, and he knew he had to share what he learned with you. Here's what Stormie had to say:

Stormie Andrews: After 29 years of marriage, I recently got divorced. I was totally shocked when my wife and "best friend" told me that she didn't love me anymore. I honestly felt we had a great marriage, and I was happy in our marriage.

Men and women see the world totally different. How could I be so completely oblivious to her feelings? It wasn't an overnight scenario, but she was feeling this way for quite some time. She was living with those feelings for a couple of years, just afraid to say anything. Meanwhile, I was oblivious to it.

Shame on me for not knowing how she felt. And shame on her for not telling me.

Dudes, listen to me. I was raised that a man had to support the family, put food on the table, and buy your wife nice things. And that's what I did. We read *The Five Love Languages* and I found out my wife didn't want the new car or fancy handbag. She wanted me to load the dishwasher, help around the house. Those were things my dad didn't do or teach me to do so, of course, I didn't do any of that.

I was completely devastated and I decided I would do anything to make our marriage work. My wife was an incredible woman who made me a better person. But the point is, it was just too late, she didn't love me anymore. My wife supported me on everyone of my dreams and goals and I feel bad that I didn't support her on her dreams. Maybe if I had noticed something early on and been more open so she could share her feelings with me, maybe we could have turned things around.

Dudes, pay attention before it's too late. Another thing I learned from my pops is we were supposed to be tough and not cry. That is simply not true, men need to cry and not hide it; it is immensely powerful. My wife gave me an incredible gift of self-discovery. I learned how important it is to be in the moment, I missed so many opportunities with my family because I was focused on work and not enjoying each and every moment with them.

Listen, *really listen* to your wife before it's too late.

A word from Dr. Joyce: The story of Stormie's marriage is heartbreaking. Losing a spouse to divorce can be devastating. But, as Stormie suggests, it often doesn't have to work out this way. Stormie very likely could have saved his marriage if only he had taken action earlier. As someone who has counseled scores of couples over the years, I can assure you that making the effort to maintain a loving, special relationship with your spouse is far more preferable than facing an *unwanted, unexpected* divorce.

Naturally, there are exceptions to the rule, but, based on my decades of experience, I tend to agree with Stormie that men and women often think differently. It's no surprise to me that John Gray's book, *Men are From Mars, Women are From Venus*, was the highest ranked work of non-fiction for nearly a decade after it was published in 1992. Women tend to place much more value on communication. When they are able to talk and share and relate with their close family and friends, women thrive.

Men, on the other hand, tend to be less open about their feelings. Whereas men think talking is about finding solutions to problems, women talk to connect and strengthen relationships. As Stormie shares above, the key for most men, then, is to learn how to become better listeners.

Dan Clark: Total Commitment

Internationally Recognized Hall of Fame Speaker

I first became aware of Dan Clark back in the mid-1980s as a result of his work speaking to motivate and give direction and purpose to the youth, a commitment which he and I share. In the last few years, I have gotten to know more about Dan and his truly exceptional work through a few mutual friends, and my involvement with the National Speakers Association, where Dan stands as one of the most active national members.

What I admire most about Dan is his integrity, his commitment to serving others, and the way he consistently puts others before himself. Dan and I also have a very similar philosophy when it comes to dealing with adversity. Dan writes that "adversity introduces us to ourselves—pain is a signal to grow, not to suffer. Once we learn the lesson the pain is teaching us the pain goes away. In life there are no mistakes, only lessons—we never lose if we always learn!"

I cannot help but be completely impressed with Dan Clark and his truly extraordinary life and career. Dan Clark is one of the world's top motivational speakers. Along with authoring more than 20 books, including several bestsellers, Dan is also the primary contributing author to the *Chicken Soup for the Soul* series. Dan has flown bombers and fighter jets. He's raced automobiles and dogsleds. He's ridden camels in Cairo, elephants in Thailand, and a Road King Harley across America with the Willie G. Davidson family. He even touched the heavens in a U2 reconnaissance aircraft.

Dan Clark has done it all.

Dan likes to create as many "once in a lifetime" opportunities as he can, and when your name is Dan Clark and you're from the Mountain States, that turns out to be quite a number.

But it hasn't always been this way for Dan. In fact, Dan's big brush with disaster might help explain another important part of how he has become the superstar that he is today.

Dan's dramatic story began when he was playing football as a sophomore at the University of Utah in 1978. During a tackling drill, Dan's athletic career came to an abrupt halt when he cracked a vertebra in his neck and severed a nerve in his right shoulder. The impact left his arm dangling, his eye drooping, and, for a few hours, the future silver-tongued speaker was completely unable to talk.

Alas, the doctors left virtually no room for hope. As Dan recalls, "I visited 16 doctors around the country, and they said the most I could hope for was a 10 percent recovery... I became a recluse, an emotional wreck. It was the loneliest time of my life. All my hopes and dreams were destroyed."

Dan, however, was not having it. He is a man of commitment, and he was committed to doing everything in his power to recover. Despite the agonizing work of rehab, Dan spent countless hours in his room working to do the simplest things, such as raising his hand above his shoulder.

Miraculously, with a couple of years of intense rehab, Dan made a full recovery to the utter astonishment of his doctors. He soon started getting invitations to speak to local high school students, and the career of a world-renowned motivational speaker was born.

After cleverly orchestrating a meeting with the legendary Zig Ziglar, and then parlaying that into a 25-year long mentoring relationship, Dan is now frequently recognized as the modern day Napoleon Hill. And from where I stand, Dan Clark, still only sixty-five, is just getting started.

Michael Hauge: The Power of Your Story

Best-Selling Author and Top Hollywood Story Consultant

When I first heard that Michael Hauge would be delivering a presentation on storytelling to my local chapter of the National Speakers Association, I was thrilled. I've always loved telling stories, and listening to other great storytellers, and I couldn't wait to hear what Michael Hauge had to say. After all, a famous American story consultant and bestselling author, Michael is a legend in his field. He's known for his work with celebrity writers, producers, actors, and directors—including people like Will Smith, Julia Roberts, Jennifer Lopez, Kirsten Dunst, Charlize Theron and Morgan  Freeman. He's also the bestselling author of *Selling Your Story in 60 Seconds.* His other bestseller, *Writing Screenplays That Sell,* now in its 20th anniversary edition, is considered a "must-read" in the industry.

For weeks after listening to Michael deliver a riveting presentation, I couldn't get his ideas about storytelling out of my mind. At that point, I had already begun working on this book, and I was well aware of the power of storytelling, but I had this sense that I was looking at my own story with fresh eyes. I also had a good feeling that I would be working with Michael at some point in the near future.

More than two years and countless responsibilities later, I had nearly finished writing this book, and my mind was focused on getting it edited and published. Then, one day out of the blue, I started thinking about Michael again. For some reason, he kept returning to my thoughts.

But I realized I didn't have his contact information. I decided I would just have to wait until the next NSA meeting to find out how to reach him. However, surprisingly, within the hour…I got an email from…wait for it…Michael Hauge!

It wasn't like he and I had already been emailing each other, or I was already on one of his lists or something. I just happened to get an email from him at the very moment I was wondering how to get in touch with him. Needless to say, I immediately picked up the phone and called the number he left on his email.

At the time, I wasn't aware of all of the famous movies he has been involved with, including blockbusters like *I Am Legend, Hancock, The Karate Kid, Suicide Squad, Bright*, etc.

As soon as Michael picked up the phone, I instantly recognized his voice.

"Is this *the* Michael Hauge, the master storyteller extraordinaire?," I asked with obvious excitement.

"After listening to you speak at NSA, I bet I would recognize that voice of yours just about anywhere."

I quickly got involved with a program Michael teaches called "The Hero's Two Journeys" which is grounded in the work of the celebrated American mythologist Joseph Campbell.

As I have had the chance to dive deeper into Michael's work, I have discovered a number of important principles and parallels with my own life experience. There are two specific concepts that are closely connected to this book, which I want to share with you.

One of the key concepts that Michael discusses in his books and workshops is the importance of "emotional truth." In fact, Michael recently said, "At the heart of everything I teach and believe about storytelling is the value of emotional truth."

What really struck me was the context in which he wrote these words. Michael's wife, Vicki, the love of his life for 44 years, passed away in late January 2020. When Michael wrote those words, he was sharing his emotional truth which, at the time, was deep, heartfelt grief. Not only did I instantly feel the pain he was feeling—both because of my own experiences losing loved ones, and because of Michael's mastery as a storyteller— but I also found his courage and will to keep going to be another compelling example of the principles shared throughout this book.

Interestingly, stress is often caused by a *lack* of emotional truth. An important part of healing, therefore, begins by finding the courage to be honest about where you are and what you are facing. The point is not to be negative, or pessimistic about where you are. The point is to be *real* about where you are and, equally important, what you need to do to get from where you are to where you want to be. As Michael writes, "heroes find the courage to be honest—about themselves, their pain, their fear, their mistakes and their shortcomings. They let go of their protective identities."

The second key concept I want to share with you from his work is about finding the courage to fight. As Michael writes, "Most heroes don't begin their stories as heroic. They start out as ordinary people, or occasionally as extraordinary people, who struggle with the same longings, desires, obstacles, pain and fears that we all do. Then, in confronting whatever conflicts they must overcome, these heroes find the courage to face their fears and take the action that is necessary."

What matters, in other words, regardless of the obstacle you face, or how you see yourself now, is that you find the courage to fight. Every day is a new day and a new chance to give it everything you've got. In fact, in every minute of every hour, you have a choice to make. You can choose to surrender to your circumstances, or you can choose to give it everything you've got. In the words of President Dwight Eisenhower, "It's not the size of the dog in the fight. It's the size of the fight in the dog." And even if you don't always win, *because* you found the courage to fight, you are, writes Michael, "transformed into someone who is truly heroic," and as a result of your courage, you will also "transform the lives of those around" you.

This is the story of the heroic, Michael explains. "Their physical or emotional courage inspires those around them, just as they inspire all of us who see or hear or read their stories. By becoming heroic, they show us how we can live better, and they give us a glimpse of our own potential for courage and connection and love."

"So think about first," he continues, "what's your goal? Get very specific about your goal, the next finish line you want to cross, so you really know, 'This is what I want.'"

Once you are crystal clear about what it is that you want, then decide right now that this moment will be the beginning of your own heroic journey.

Clive Buchanan: The Value of Challenge

Keynote Speaker, Author, Consultant, and Master Herbalist

Clive Buchanan is a powerhouse. He has a commanding presence. On the speaking platform, his audiences are captivated from the moment he first begins. The former president of both the Hawaii and Utah chapters of the National Speakers Association, Clive has clearly mastered the craft of professional speaking.

What really stands out for me, however, and what really sets Clive apart, other than his heartfelt commitment to helping his audiences, is that Clive Buchanan is a master storyteller. And, boy, does he have a story to tell (as you'll see below).

I first met Clive when he visited the Las Vegas chapter of the National Speakers Association a few years ago. Instantly, I could feel his energy and sense his compassion. A man of high purpose, we clicked right away and have been friends ever since.

There are a number of things I admire about Clive, including his talent as an author—his book, *18 Steps to Greatness*, which is based on Clive's three decades of studying the success literature, is simply *outstanding*. I've also long been impressed with Clive's business acumen as a speaker, trainer, consultant and coach. But if you want to know what I most admire about Clive, you have to hear his story for yourself, and here it is in Clive's own words:

The Value of Challenge

I was on the Delta airplane, on the way to Nashville for the most important meeting and convention I thought I would ever attend, when my feet began to tingle again. This time it was different. By the time I arrived in Nashville, my feet felt like they were asleep. They were numb and getting more numb. I prayed they would take back to normal by the time the convention started the next day.

Morning came and to my dismay, my feet were still asleep and there was now tingling in my legs. As the day progressed, my legs began to get numb. Fear set in. I needed help walking. By the end of the convention, there was no improvement. My hands were beginning to tingle. That night I was in near panic, wondering if I could get home, the next day. Have you ever felt this kind of panic?

The trip home was uneventful. Hands, legs, and feet all numb. I could still use my limbs, but I could not feel them. Doctor visits and tests followed. Blood tests, CAT scans, spinal taps, and dexterity tests were all part of the mix. After six weeks of anxiety, I received the diagnosis, secondary progressive multiple sclerosis, commonly called MS.

My doctor immediately recognized that most of my problems were symptoms of MS. However, he ran tests for cancer, tumors, strokes, and other conditions, in addition to the ones for MS for safety sake.

When I got the confirmation that I had MS, I was relieved. It was good to know it was not all in my head.

Little did I know at this time that this tragedy would become a great blessing. Looking at my history, the doctor concluded that I first showed symptoms in my early twenties, but they had been misdiagnosed. About age 23, I started having strange maladies. When my leg dragged, the doctor always blamed it on the bullet that was in my leg from an accident in my youth. When I had double vision, the doctor blamed it on the explosion and glass in my eyes that left me blind for a couple of weeks. When I became tired and fatigued when I got overheated, the doctor blamed it on the family ticker.

Our family has a history of heart and cardiovascular conditions. My mother died of a heart condition when she was 43 and my father died of a heart attack at the age of 48. The explanations for my symptoms were so good, neither my doctors nor I thought to look for another cause. I had symptoms for over 17 years before I was diagnosed with Multiple Sclerosis (MS).

I asked the doctor for a prognosis. Based on my history of relapsing remitting symptoms followed by a consistent increase in symptoms he thought I had secondary progressive MS. He said my condition would slowly deteriorate. His prediction was grim at best.

A few weeks later, an old friend came to visit me. When she saw my condition, she was shocked. My speech was so slurred she had trouble understanding me. My arms, legs and head were shaking non-stop. It was so hard for her to see a close friend in this condition that she could not bring herself to come to my side of the room.

When she left, I resolved that I would walk again. I got the doctor on the phone and demanded a cure. After a long argument he said, "Clive you must accept the fact that you are going to spend the rest of your life watching TV with someone else changing the channels." His comments and attitude made me even more determined to walk.

Later that day, when I was all alone, using all the mind power I could muster, I forced myself to my feet. I stood straight and tall and attempted to walk. As my body began to move forward, I realized my feet were not moving. I tried to bring my arms forward to break my fall, but they did not move. I fell hard, and on my face.

There, on the family room floor, somewhat dazed, I saw, what I perceived to be, a vision. I saw myself standing in front of huge audiences, teaching that in this life it does not matter what happens to you. It matters how you respond to it. You might not control everything or everyone around you, but you do control how you respond. I was teaching that you and everyone you know has or will have a condition or trial that is the equivalent of my MS.

The vision continued. A stage curtain dropped, and then opened again, as I began to teach a new message. You must take responsibility for your own life. You should not blame anyone for your problems or give anyone the credit for your achievements. Everything is up to you and God. Get the best information you can find, then make your own decisions. If you do not like something either change it or change your attitude.

Finally, the curtain dropped, and opened once more. This time I was extolling the virtues of holistic health. I was teaching how to get the best from herbs, food supplements, and conventional medicine. That communication skills, success, and leadership are all necessary for the best mental, physical, and spiritual heath. You and thousands like you were there in the audience.

At that instant in time, over thirty-five years ago, my whole life changed forever. What seemed like a curse and very unfair, led to a wonderful life and an opportunity to help thousands around the world.

As the vision faded, and I began to come to myself, my mind was filled with the supplements, mind games, and exercises necessary to overcome Multiple Sclerosis. Miraculously, within less than a month, the visible symptoms of MS were gone.

I still needed a walking stick to help with balance for about three years, but I was healed. I had overcome MS. To this day, I can walk and talk and move around as if nothing ever happened.

I have been asked many times to explain how I overcame MS, and which supplements or drugs I use. (It should be pointed out, I still technically have MS, but MS does not have me. I am symptom free.) I use no drugs in my MS regimen. The book, *One Man's Victory*, explains the full program I followed.

In the years following my miraculous recovery, I had the opportunity to speak to groups large and small. I was a guest on radio programs heard around the world. Mark Victor Hansen, Art Berg, Brian Tracy, Kathy Loveless, Zig Ziglar, and others in the speaking field became my friends and mentors. Doctors Jack Richason, Stan Malstrom, Bernard Jenson, John Cristopher, and many others mentored me in the holistic health fields.

Dr. Joyce Brown, the author of this book, is incredibly special to me. She has overcome challenges that would have stopped or discouraged most people. She motivates me to do more. Her quest to stop suicide is both noble and necessary. During my worst times, as Multiple Sclerosis progressed, I often thought of suicide. Her single question, "Do you know what is on the other side?" would have put an end to those thoughts.

You, who read this book, have more potential than you can imagine. Will you become great or famous? Who knows? The fact that you will touch and change other people's lives is a given. Will they remember you as the one who just gave up or the one who kept getting up, even after colossal failure. Books like **18 Steps to Greatness** can give you tools to achieve more, but it is up to you to determine what you become. Every person who has ever made a significant difference in other people's lives has failed and been knocked down many times. It is the art of getting up after being knocked down or failing that makes you strong.

When challenges and trials come know that there is always a blessing that is greater than the challenge. Sometimes you must look hard to find it and it is often delayed. You, my friend, make a difference and the world is better because you are here.

Jim Quick: The Miracle Power of Prayer

After my husband Earl died, I decided I needed to sell the house we had in California. While staying there, I began praying and asking God what I was supposed to do next.

Before long, it was clear that I was to start a non-profit organization. I picked up the North San Bernardino phone book and began flipping through the pages. When I happened upon Jim's ad in the yellow pages I felt prompted to call. I knew this was whom I was supposed to go see.

When I first went to his office and we met, I immediately had this feeling that he and I were old friends. When I told him I found his listing in the phone book, he said he didn't think he had a listing in the phone book. We both burst into laughter.

As we sat and discussed the details of the non-profit organization I had in mind, I knew that Jim and I were supposed to meet. I was very impressed with Jim's credentials as an Enrolled Agent (EA) with the U.S. Department of the Treasury, as well as his extraordinary knowledge and experience (Jim has worked with over 200 non-profit organizations, many with budgets exceeding $50 million).

What really won me over though was how much Jim believed in our cause and our shared belief in God. Jim and I quickly grew to become good friends. He has now been shepherding Stress and Grief Relief, Inc for more than 20 years and, over that time, he has helped us to stay on the right course with his wise counsel, encouragement, and commitment to our cause. What follows is Jim's miraculous story in his own words:

Jim Quick: "The doctor's assessment was devastating. Hearing those words "Parkinson's Disease" created panic for me. I had known I was having trouble holding a pencil, and dropping things, but this diagnosis reinforced that awful fear that had haunted me for the past month. As a former hospital controller, I had access to great medical professionals…this friend who diagnosed me just happened to be the chairman of the department of neurology at a nationally recognized school of medicine. This diagnosis was given to me in March of 2005.

By August of 2005, I could only stay out of bed for an hour at a time, feeling totally exhausted. The tremors were awful. My son-in-law decided to move us to Northern California so they could take care of me and my wife until I passed.

But God had a greater idea! On November 3rd, 2005, a good friend (a truck driver) was passing through our town, and asked me and my wife to join him at Sheri's Restaurant in Red Bluff, California for lunch. While we were eating, I kept dropping my fork...it was embarrassing. He took my hand and prayed, "Lord, take these tremors away." At that very moment, the tremors ceased, and to this day, I haven't had another tremor. My life was restored.

I still get great joy when my doctor friends call me, asking me if the tremors have returned. With GREAT joy I tell them that God doesn't make mistakes....His work is ALWAYS perfect!"

Aimmee Kodachian: Focus on the Light

Author, Keynote Speaker, Founder and Host
of the "Empowering Humanity" TV Show

I first met Aimmee Kodachian when I was a guest on the World of Book Reviews television show with host Judi Moreo. Aimmee is the producer of the show, which is part of the

Armount TV network, and which is produced in a state-of-the-art facility and studio set in Las Vegas, Nevada. I was invited on the show to discuss my book, *God's Heavenly Answers*. While I was on the set, I had the opportunity to meet a few of the studio executives, including Aimmee.

Aimmee immediately struck me as a savvy business professional, but she was also so warm and caring. I liked her instantly. Before long, I started seeing both Aimmee and Judi at business conferences and events in the greater Las Vegas area, and we quickly became friends. Along with her powerful, persevering faith, the thing that I admire most about Aimmee is her courage. As you'll see in her story below, no matter how challenging her situation, Aimmee is fearless about facing the reality of it, and then finding a way to learn and grow from it and, ultimately, break through. This brings me to one of my other favorite things about Aimmee. Whatever lessons she does learn from her experience, Aimmee is always looking for ways to share that wisdom with others so that they may grow and thrive as well.

Aimmee Kodachian's book *Tears of Hope* is so inspiring and motivational, and I'm eagerly looking forward to her upcoming movie, *Light from the Shadows*.

As you will learn from her story, Aimmee's hope, determination, sense of purpose, and profound faith and trust in God enabled her not merely to endure the terrible trials and extreme hardships of her life, but to transform those experiences and rebuild her life in such a way that she is now a glowing example for countless others around the world.

Since our first meeting in the Las Vegas television studio, Aimmee and I have become very good friends. I recently had a chance to catch up with her, and talk about her life story growing up in Lebanon with her family and four brothers, and her miraculous transformation from a single mother living in a war-torn nation to the wonderful and successful businesswoman that she is today. What follows is based on our interview:

Since the age of seven, Aimmee was carrying a dark secret of being sexually, physically, and emotionally abused by her brother Elie. School was very difficult for her as she was dealing with severe dyslexia. She was constantly made fun of and bullied. Aimmee was 12 years old when the 1975 Lebanese Civil War began.

Early in the conflict, a bomb hit the Kodachian home, and Aimmee watched as her favorite brother was killed right before her eyes. Instantly, the Kodachian's lost everything and became homeless.

"My family decided to send me and my six-year-old brother, Roger, to an old boarding school in the mountains for safety. My heart went with my parents as I watched them drive away, leaving us behind. I didn't know if I would ever see them or hear their voices again. There was no phone, and the roads were impassable. I had no mentor and no shoulder to cry on.

"Food was in short supply there, and we had no electricity or running water. My six-year-old brother, Roger would dig through the garbage to find scraps of food to eat. I could feel and see his broken heart. Tears would run down his cheeks as he asked me about Mom and the rest of the family.

"I had no choice but to be strong for my brother and take on the role of mother. I would comfort him and share with him the small amount of food I was given. I was losing hope, scared, confused, and devastated by the idea that we might not see our family again.

"I felt powerless, afraid, and alone. My heart filled with darkness. One afternoon I sat down on the bench and leaned my back against a tree. Then I took a deep breath, opened my heart, and I completely surrendered to the one thing I knew was bigger than the darkness. I looked up and asked God, the loving and caring Creator I'd been raised to believe was there for us, to help me.

"At that moment, the feeling of darkness was replaced and filled with light. Then, I heard and felt His voice in a very unique and different way, one I never heard or felt before, telling me that everything was going to be okay. Somehow, I felt the harmony flowing between my heart, mind, soul, and my intuition as they were connected. My spirit lifted, and I experienced a deeper spiritual connection. I could feel the presence of God.

"Several months later, I was united with my family, but our lives were never the same. Due to my severe dyslexia and the war, I was forced to leave school after the 4th grade. My dream of becoming a teacher was fading away. My mother was covering her pain with medication," Aimmee said.

"Aimmee," her mother told her, "it's best for you to get married. You have no hope to go back to school or an opportunity to find a job."

"Living with an abusive brother was difficult. I desperately needed to get away from Elie. My mother's suggestion to get married was not a bad idea; after all, I told myself. I walked down the aisle just a few days after my 14th birthday and started a new life with my husband's family, where I was not welcomed. I gave birth to my beautiful daughter, Silva, at 15. When I first laid eyes on her and held her in my arms, I felt I was given a very special and precious gift and a reason to live."

"Later, my husband left the country unannounced, and I became a single mother before I turned 19 in a culture that had no room and no sympathy for divorced women back then. I lived through the war for 13 years, escaped death several times, and lost many family members. In the meantime, I was perfecting and learning how to stay connected, to God and paid very close attention to the source of my thoughts," Aimmee said.

In 1988, Aimmee got the opportunity to come to the United States. Despite not knowing English, having only a 4th-grade education, severe dyslexia, and less than $200 in her pocket, Aimmee knew the situation in America had to be better than war-torn Lebanon.

Unfortunately, not knowing the language here turned out to be a major hurdle, and Aimmee and her daughter ended up homeless. Despite being repeatedly told she could not make it here and that she needed to go back home where she had family and spoke the language, she was determined to make it in America. While sleeping on couches and in closets, she turned her Fear to Faith and started to do everything she could to educate herself and learn English.

A couple of years later, Aimmee met and married a loving and caring all-around American family guy named Tom. Her husband soon discovered that she had an entrepreneurial mind that he always wished to have. Tom was so proud to see Aimmee become a successful entrepreneur.

After writing a book about her experience in the war, Aimmee started to find her purpose. She began to think about all that she had learned, how she had survived one nightmare scenario after another, and how she could use her experience to help others.

Today, along with being a keynote speaker, and ambassador for peace, Aimmee Kodachian is the founder, creator, and host of the "Empowering Humanity" TV Show where she interviews experts around the world, including guests such as the internationally acclaimed author and speaker Judi Moreo; former Nevada Attorney General George Chanos; and keynote speakers such as SoFeya Joseph, former Olympic coach, author, and international speaker;

and "Law of Attraction" teacher, Bob Doyle, who was featured in the blockbuster movie *The Secret.*

Now, award-winning screenwriter Eric P. Granger has adapted Aimmee's book, Tears of Hope, into a motion picture entitled Light from the Shadows, which has a strong message for humanity about love, forgiveness, hope, and peace."

When Aimmee looks back on her life for lessons she can pass on to others, she returns to a few key themes again and again. First, Aimmee says, "You must focus on seeing the light in the midst of the darkness. Sometimes there is so much darkness in our lives that we don't see the light. The light is always there, but we miss it because we're only looking at the darkness. In order to see the light, we first have to surrender. When we surrender to God," she says, "then we can start to focus more on the wisdom and insights that we are learning when we are going through the darkness. In fact," says Aimmee, "the dark or difficult place is very often the place where we learn. When we are going through the darkness, we stretch and grow our muscles, emotionally and spiritually, bringing us to a different place. That's when we see difficult situation from a different perspective and overcome it."

The second key theme Aimmee discussed is the importance of taking an overall positive view of our experience, including our most challenging obstacles and setbacks. Rather than looking at a difficult situation as "something that is happening to me," Aimmee added, far better to understand it as "something that is happening for me." When you do this, then your perspective will change, and you will be open to the wisdom and insight you can gain from the experience, no matter how difficult. In the words of the ancient Greek poet Aeschylus, "Even in our sleep, pain which cannot forget falls drop by drop upon the heart, until, in our own despair, against our will, comes wisdom through the awful grace of God."

Another critical lesson Aimmee shares with her audiences is the importance of recognizing your unique gifts. Too often, people think they have to be different, or become different to be successful.

But what people really need to do is "see and absorb" the truth of the gifts that God has already given them. The solution, in other words, is not to be somebody else. The solution is to recognize your own unique and amazing gifts and be your own exceptional and wonderful self. As Aimmee often puts it, "You don't have to be perfect to be beautiful and powerful. All you have to do is be yourself."

Too many people ignore this, but, she said, "If we are not respecting ourselves, then we're not respecting what God gave us." When you start to really understand and appreciate and use the gifts God gave you, then you start to move from surviving to thriving.

Finally, Aimmee says, we have to take responsibility for our lives. The world can be ugly at times, but to blame God is to miss the point. Instead of throwing up our hands and crying out, "Where is God?" she said, "We need to focus on doing our part." We all have a role to play in making this a better world. "We all have a purpose for being here. God gave us the gifts that He gave us because He wants us to use them."

Aimmee's mission is to empower and elevate humanity's consciousness through education and inspiration so they can have hope and see the light through darkness.

Anthony DeNino: Trust and Believe

Author, Keynote Speaker, Founder and
President of CORe— Creating Our Reality™

I first met Anthony DeNino as I was leaving the ALS conference in Salt Lake City in 2019. He was hosting a booth as part of an annual symposium for the National Partnership for Juvenile Services (NPJS). He and I struck up a nice conversation

and I soon learned that he works with non-profit organizations. We also found that we had other interests in common, including working with youth. I gave him a copy of my book, *God's Heavenly Answers*, and we discussed the possibility of working together on various online marketing projects for Stress and Grief Relief, Inc. We've been working together ever since, and I now consider him a good friend.

There are many things I admire about Anthony. He is caring, consistent, dependable, genuine, and sincere. But what I admire most is how in-tune he is with God, and how he focuses on relationships, and how to help people grow. Not surprisingly, these characteristics combine to make Anthony a very successful leader, speaker, workshop facilitator, and entrepreneur (he is the President and Founder of CORe—Creating Our Reality, Inc.).

Anthony has an interesting story to share with you, and, as you might imagine after reading about my story, I very much relate to the personal experience he shares with you below. In fact, beyond my own experience, I have encountered a number of people who have received tremendous, life-changing benefits through prayer and meditation. If you have ever been curious about this practice, you are really going to appreciate Anthony's story.

Anthony DeNino: "What are you doing?" "You're hurting your wife?" "She's finally going to say 'enough-is-enough' and leave you!" "Just get another job and suck it up!" "You're not smart enough to do this."

These are just a handful of the thoughts that would run through my head on a daily basis after starting my own company. No guaranteed paycheck, no benefits, credit cards getting closer and closer to their limits…Meanwhile, my older daughter was getting ready to go off to college, out-of-state, meaning an even higher tuition bill.

Starting a business is like having children. There really is no perfect time to do either. But I'm pretty sure I started my business at the *worst possible* time.

Sure, I was beginning to drum up some business as a speaker, and I was able to do some workshops for a couple of companies. The problem was that there was nothing I could count on. There was no consistency. And because nobody knew me and trusted I could deliver, the fees I was earning for these gigs was awfully low.

So there I was, a motivational speaker who didn't believe what he was saying for his own life. Of course, I could talk-the-talk. In fact, externally, I was fine. Internally, however, I was a mess.

It started a few years before I had gone out on my own, but now it was coming to a head. I knew I had to get myself out of this funk. But how? How could I overcome my own negative, self-defeating thoughts?

Suddenly, one day it happened. I was just getting into meditation at the time, and I recalled a Wayne Dyer quote. "If I don't go within, I go without." So, that's exactly what I did. I really focused on going within. I was determined to learn what it was that was causing me to have these doubts and fears.

Ultimately, through meditation and prayer, I came to realize what was at the root of all of my fear.

It was so obvious. In fact, I knew it all along, but I just never let myself admit it. I was, after all, a good Catholic kid from New York. I went to church. I believed in God. And I always felt He was leading the way. I was thankful for all that I did have too. Heck, I even wrote a book on the topic, *The Power of Giving and Gratitude! A Path To Creating Your Reality* (which, *speaking of gratitude*, I had the good fortune of sharing on a recent television interview).

Yet, somehow, despite all this, I wouldn't admit the truth.

And the truth was…I never *fully* trusted.

I could never *fully* let go.

As with the outward confidence and beliefs, there was a certain level of trust…how could I not trust God, the Creator of the Universe, the Alpha and the Omega…but did I really trust Him all the way through?

Prior to going out on my own, I had prayed for answers as to whether I should give up the security of a job and paycheck for the freedom and flexibility to do things my way—to grow something from nothing, to positively impact people around the world through my speaking, workshops, and books. And I was truly blessed—all signs pointed to "Yes!"

But now I was at this point where I realized I didn't fully trust that it would happen, and it was significantly undermining my confidence and resolve.

So how did I overcome it?

I went deep into meditation and asked just one question, "Why won't I fully trust and let go?"

What's interesting is that, *somehow*, I got myself into the deepest meditative state I have ever experienced. Then, once there, I asked God my burning question. To be clear, I wasn't really asking,

"Why won't I fully trust..." What I was really asking was, "Why won't I fully trust YOU..."

And amazingly, miraculously, I heard His answer. It wasn't this big, booming voice, the voice we often imagine God would have. It was more like a still, silent voice. Nevertheless, I received the message loud and clear,

"Trust.

Always Trust Me.

Now and Forever.

Believe in Me and I Believe in You.

Trust.

Love,

God"

As I came out of meditation, all I could think was, "WOW!" Words like amazing, incredible, and unbelievable came to mind. It was beautiful, and, as clear and simple as it was, it was so profoundly helpful.

Of course, I still slip into moments of doubt on occasion, but never to the extreme that it once was.

Today, I am now fully immersed in my work with a much more profound understanding and deep appreciation for the fact that I was put on this path for a reason, for many reasons actually, some of which are clear. Now, as a result of this profound personal experience, my work, my purpose is unquestionably clear.

Now, with a heartfelt sense of gratitude and wonder and awe, I can report that this incident marked a real turning point in my career. It didn't happen overnight, of course, but gradually the number of workshops and trainings I do for companies and nonprofits increased. I started to receive invitations to be the keynote speaker at national conferences. And the consulting work I do has taken off. I even started my own podcast show, "Tales From The SMART Side—Successful Strategies For Businesses and NPOs."

As excited as I am about all that has been happening, I'm not sharing this to get you to look at me. I'm sharing this to get you to look at Him. Because this story isn't really about me. It's about you, and your relationship with Him. It's about you going deep, and getting the answers to your own burning questions, and, thereby, moving forward with your own life purpose and goals.

Dr. Vern Kilbourn: Willpower and Grit

Dr. Vern Kilbourn and his wife, Barbara, have been members of Toastmasters International for many years, and, since our first meeting together, we have become very good friends. They are both such caring and loving people. I still remember how they helped me to get to the competition that I won when I was competing in the Southern Utah Toastmasters contest.

One of the things I admire most about Dr. Kilbourn is his determination. Far too many doctors today are all too ready to say, "I'm sorry, but nothing more can be done." Dr. Kilbourn stands in stark contrast to this hopeless attitude and, not surprisingly, he gets indisputable outcomes as a result.

I also admire how extraordinarily knowledgeable he is about health and medicine. He has a remarkable depth to his understanding of healthcare and the intimate, inextricable link between proper healthcare and effective self-care.

Dr. Kilbourn also happens to deliver a powerful talk about healthcare that would be amazing to have recorded to share with the world, perhaps for YouTube or even a TED Talk. It's just fantastic. The following is Dr. Kilbourn's miraculous story in his own words:

Dr. Vern Kilbourn: There was a time in my life when I felt I had descended into "The Depths of Hell." I had been flying a hang glider at "Point of the Mountain," in the south end of Salt Lake Valley. In order to prevent a midair collision with another glider I turned while flying too slowly. The glider "stalled out" and I crashed into the side of the mountain.

I was severely injured. I did not lose consciousness, but I could not move or feel anything below my neck. I could talk in low voice and move my eyes. I could breathe very lightly. Several people came to my aid as they had witnessed the crash. They were attempting to get me out of the harness attached to the glider. They cut the straps rather than trying to move me. I cautioned them about moving me very much. Being a Chiropractic Physician, I knew my spine was badly damaged. One of the people lifted my right arm to reposition it and I could see there were several fractures. The ambulance crew arrived in about twenty minutes and provided splints, a neck brace and a back board. The ambulance crews at that time were not paramedics. They did not have extensive training.

I was carried off the mountain and loaded into the ambulance. They were taking me to St. Marks Hospital in Salt Lake City. I had the driver use a radio telephone to call my good friend Dr. Powell in Salt Lake City (cell phones were not in use at the time). I explained to Dr. Powell that I had been in an accident and had spinal injury and other fractures. I requested his help as a neurosurgeon and requested an orthopedic doctor of his choosing. Dr. Powell reminded me that he practiced at Holy Cross Hospital in Downtown. I told the ambulance people to take me to that hospital. They said I might not live that long. I exclaimed "what the hell," if death is that close it won't make a difference anyway. Upon arrival at Holy Cross, Dr. Powell and Dr. Carson were waiting at the door. Testing and examination started immediately. Dr. Powell gave me an injection of medication to inhibit swelling of the spinal cord. X-rays were taken of my spine, body, and right arm. The initial examination revealed two vertebral fractures, C-5 and C-6, multiple fractures of the right forearm, left clavicle, and several ribs.

Two holes were drilled into my head, and steel pegs driven into the holes. Ten pound weights were attached to each peg. I was then strapped to a nylon web frame work called a Striker Frame. I would be in this position for 2 hours. Then, a frame exactly like the bottom frame would be placed on the front of me. I would then be rotated where I would be looking at the floor. Every two hours for 24 hours a day I would be looking at either the floor or the ceiling. Normally this procedure required three people. With me, 6 people were required. My right arm was in a cast, the ten pound traction weights and I-V tubes and drain tubes had to be moved from one position to the other.

This program was followed for 8 weeks, giving the fractures time to heal, after which I was taken off the Striker Frame and placed in a regular hospital bed. I was still paralyzed from my neck down.

M.R.I. machines were not in use and CT scans were not available. X-rays do not show spinal cord injury. It was not known how much damage had occurred. Myelograms were the only way to assess damage. The procedure requires a dye to be injected into the spinal fluid. The patient is in prone position. The patient is then tilted up or down with X-rays taken at intervals. The dye collects in voids or torn areas of the spinal cord. The dye shows on X-rays. The test was to be done in my room with a portable X-ray unit.

After the dye was injected the portable X-ray machine malfunctioned. I was moved onto a gurney and transported to the X-ray lab. The dye was dispersed in several areas of my spine and was not able to be retrieved when attempted. I still have after forty years worth of pools of dye around the foramen magnum, the area of the cervical fractures and the sacral area of the spinal cord. This causes frequent inflammation and pain.

The test was botched, but did reveal serious spinal cord damage, and I could probably remain a quadriplegic for the rest of my life.

When I was given this information I spiraled into a depression. My life was gone. I had no money. I could not work. I had no home. Nine years of college, and seventeen years of building my practice as a Chiropractic Physician were all down the drain.

I had gone through a divorce and was paying alimony and child support for seven children. I never told my children the reason for the divorce [which was??]. I did not want them to lose respect for their mother. As a result, I was hated by them. During the four plus months I spent in the hospital, two of my children came once.

Arrangements were being made for me to be transferred to a long-term military facility. These things take time. On Halloween day a nurse was feeding me breakfast. I don't know what belief she endorsed but she believed that any person that died in the hospital had their spirit come back to the hospital on Halloween to roam the halls. She was not paying attention to me. She was looking out in the hallway, and in the corners of the room. By the time breakfast was over I had oatmeal in my eyes, eyebrows, ears, mustache, beard and down my neck. I screamed inside myself "by the God above, I will not live this way! I will either walk out of this hospital or I will find a way to take my life."

From the moment of that declaration I spent my days and nights willing my body to move. I pictured myself marching and actually counting cadence, 'Hut one, two, thee, four..,' over and over again. Moving my head and neck and into my shoulders as much as possible. I pictured my feet and hips moving with the rhythm. Several *weeks* later, I thought I felt movement in my left big toe. I asked a nurse if it moved? She let out a scream that echoed down the hall: "Doc can move a toe!"

Up to that time, not very much had been done with rehabilitation. The expectations were to keep the patient comfortable, try standing up with a slant table, or sit in a wheelchair. Life expectancy for a quadriplegic was 5 to 7 years. It took a celebrity like Christopher Reeve to change expectations.

As movement increased, exercise started in earnest. When I was asked to do ten, I did twenty more when I got back to my room. I had to learn to walk again. I had to develop balance. Muscles and tissues had to be rebuilt. I had to build strength.

The first three months in the hospital I lost 90 pounds of weight (Weight Watchers, eat your heart out). I don't recommend this way to lose weight. The weight loss was mostly from what is called "disuse atrophy." Slowly and steadily function returned. There were times when I got discouraged. I did not think things were improving as fast as I wanted. I was able to get out of bed and shuffle around the room. From my room on the 3rd floor, I could see the tops of evergreen trees next to the building. I determined that it would be possible to open the window and crawl out. After evaluating everything, I decided that, with my luck, my fall would be cushioned by the shrubbery and I would only acquire more injuries.

My attitude about continuing with rehabilitation was reinforced by a patient coming back to the hospital. He had been a patient several years earlier. He was involved in an automobile accident that left him being a paraplegic. After many weeks of rehab and being fitted with leg braces, he could get out of a wheelchair and use crutches to get around. He was given disability, and provided living facilities. He had a live-in girlfriend, and things were going well.

The girlfriend, however, decided to steal the disability checks for her own use. The man became depressed and decided to end his life. He did not know anatomy well enough to accomplish the goal. When putting the pistol to his head the bullet only severed both optic nerves. He was now a blind paraplegic.

After being hospitalized for sixteen weeks my right arm was still in a cast. The cast was cumbersome and interfering with rehabilitation. I called attention to the fact the bones in the forearm were not healing. The doctor asked how I knew, no recent X-rays had been taken. I pointed out that when the hang glider crashed my right thumb was smashed. The thumbnail was black.

After sixteen weeks there should have been some healing. When nerves are damaged function is lost and so is healing. X-rays were taken and confirmed my suspicion. There was absolutely no indication of healing. I was advised that amputation just below the elbow was recommended. I asked about options. Metal plates could be attached to the larger pieces of bone to stabilize the arm and the cast could be removed.

I chose this option. Two plates called "European Plates" were surgically implanted in my right forearm. The plates are shaped like pieces of tubing cut long-ways. Each plate was attached to a separate bone. One to the Radius and one to the Ulna. Surgical steel screws were used for the attachment. The surgery went well until in the recovery room. An overzealous nurse overdosed me on Demoral and caused cardiac arrest. I woke up two days later in the I.C.U.

The plates eventually helped the healing process. It took about 6 years for all of the nonunion fractures to heal (a fact questioned by some orthopedists). These plates will remain in my arm for the rest of my life.

After four and one half months, I was released from the hospital and went to live with my fiancé. She made arrangements in her home for me to stay while continuing my rehabilitation. Eventually I was able to drive and went to work partial days. I was soon able to drive and resume some of my usual activities.

The process of rehabilitation from paralysis is not a fast nor easy thing. It takes days, months and years. As time passed I was able to return to a somewhat normal life. I got married, started working full time and resumed all recreational activities, including snowmobiling, motorcycles, ATVs, swimming, and whitewater river running. I renewed and completed recertification of my private pilot license. I resumed operating machinery and heavy equipment. I owned and operated a dump truck, a Caterpillar bulldozer, a backhoe tractor, and a front end loader.

I am providing information about these things in my life to give you some perspective on what can be accomplished with determination and effort. I have faced many challenges before and after the hang-gliding accident. There have been at least fifteen times in my life I could have died. Five of those times were from drowning.

I will not at this time give an account of them. It is not the time or place. The purpose of this commentary for Dr. Joyce Brown's book is to reinforce her message about suicide prevention. What a TRAGEDY to be losing so many lives, particularly our young people. We must find a way to reach out to people so they understand that killing yourselves is not the right answer. It is the wrong answer, and one that cannot be reversed. It is an answer that psychologically kills the people around you that love and care about you.

If I had given up on that Halloween day 43 years ago, I would have lost 43 years of the best time of my life. I am, at the time of this writing, 86 years old. I am in my 3rd and final marriage.

During this past 43 years, I have traveled to most parts of the world. I have met and mingled with hundreds of people. Some of them didn't like me. I didn't like some of them. When I was single and dating I was interested in several ladies for matrimony. They turned me down. Thank goodness. Otherwise, I would not have found the right one. My point to everyone is this: there are very few things in this life worth killing yourselves for. Bad grades, loss of a boyfriend or girlfriend, an insult on Facebook, loss of a job, none of these are reason enough to take your life. I have been there, and done that more than once plus more things. Before you consider doing anything regrettable, remember the council given by Dr. Joyce.

"Are you sure anything is going to be any better when you leave this life? Are you sure you will not face the same problem there if you don't solve it here?"

PLEASE GET HELP
God Bless everyone.
Sincerely,
Dr. Vern Kilbourn. D.C.

Dr. William Moulton:
A Small Tooth, But a Big Difference

Dr. William Moulton and his wife, Janeen, have been very dear friends of mine for the last several years. I had long been reading Dr. Moulton's attention-grabbing articles on homeopathy and holistic dentistry in the Desert Valley Times in Mesquite, Nevada. His knowledge in these fields, along with acupuncture, was so impressive and extensive that I began referring people to him. To this day, Dr. Moulton and Janeen remain great friends and encouragers to me and the work of our non-profit.

Dr. Moulton has known about my story of having been healed of ALS, and he agreed to share a story from his professional practice. The following is his own account of one of his patients who recovered from ALS.

Dr. William Moulton: Hi, I'm Dr. William Moulton, D.D.S. I practice in Las Vegas, Nevada and have provided dental care for the patients of homeopathic physicians in our city since 1988. There are three types of problems that can arise from dental materials, according to homeopathic dentists: toxins, allergies and electrical emissions that can interfere with your meridians. There are other issues with root canals and extractions we won't deal with right now. I have gotten a lot of positive feedback from my patients, but my most dramatic experiences have been related to amalgam fillings.

One patient in 1992, named Michelle, who was diagnosed with ALS, was given one year to live. She desperately researched therapies and read that mercury could be a contributing factor, so she made an appointment with me to remove her silver amalgam fillings which generally consist of 50% mercury in a perpetually volatile state.

When she first came in to my office, she could barely walk or talk. When removing her amalgams and replacing them with composite fillings or non-metal crowns, we had to follow a specific protocol to prevent exposing her to additional mercury and other negative effects. On her last day in our office, her speech was normal and she literally skipped out the door.

She went back to her physician and he was baffled as he said that she no longer had ALS. Channel 13 did a documentary on her, but I did not let them use my name because back then other dentists frowned on anybody claiming their fillings were toxic. Today, most but not all fillings are composite, and nobody cares if you remove amalgams.

To this day, Michelle is perfectly normal, but there are other issues we need to consider before concluding that removing mercury fillings would be a cure-all for ALS. For one thing, although mercury is a neurotoxin, it does not just dissipate from your body like vitamins or alcohol. It is retained indefinitely and is very difficult to remove. In order for Michelle to have such immediate results, it might have been from some other change that had occurred, because she still had the same amount of mercury in her body that had accumulated up to that point. Some homeopaths consider that the most harm derived from metal fillings is actually the electrical current that they can produce. The body actually has a natural electrical system of its own. Some people might still be skeptical about acupuncture meridians, but in spite of their ancient discovery they have been scientifically proven to exist. They are even used to monitor the heart and other biological functions. These currents run directly through each of your teeth, but the voltage is extremely low. In comparison, the electrical current produced by dissimilar metals in an electrolyte, like saliva, can be thousands of times greater. I have just described a galvanic reaction similar to what occurs in a car battery. Whether that interference with your natural circuitry has a physiological effect is arguable, but anecdotal evidence of relationships between measurable current along specific meridians associated with pathology abounds. Take acupuncture therapy for instance. There are reams of proof that these circuits can be enhanced or altered. In order for Michelle to have such an immediate response, it might have been from some other more immediately changed condition, such as electrical interference, because she still had the same amount of mercury in her body that had accumulated up to that point. Another consideration is that ALS is actually a blanket diagnosis for one or more items of a list of symptoms for which the cause(s) are unknown. So, like Chronic Fatigue Syndrome, it could have any number of causes. That's what makes it so difficult. You just have to keep trying, like Michelle did.

A word from Dr. Joyce: I have great respect for, and highly recommend Dr. Moulton as a holistic dentist. I'm so appreciative of his willingness to share Michelle's miraculous story. I agree that it is important to consider the other possible explanations for such a rapid recovery. What I find so compelling about her story is the timing, and that her recovery from ALS coincided so directly with the removal of her mercury-amalgam fillings. Her story is also congruent with the revelation I received on the Other Side, concerning mercury-amalgam fillings, as well as the personal testimonies of scores of people I have met or heard from over the years since my near-death experience in 1983.

Dr. Moulton and I have discussed this further, and, along with considerable scientific support, we both agree that there are clear advantages of getting the amalgam fillings removed—including allowing the immune system to fight whatever else is going on, instead of having to constantly battle the effects of the continued release of mercury vapor as you chew or grind your teeth. But remember, if you do have your mercury-amalgam fillings removed, it's very important to have them taken out in the proper way (i.e. using a "dental dam" to prevent any particles from leaking down the throat during the procedure), as Dr. Moulton does in his dental practice.

David Bennett: Transforming Perspective

Speaker, Author, IANDS Board Member at Large,
Consultant for numerous radio and television
programs, including Oprah and Dr. Oz

Being a member of IANDS, I became acquainted with David Bennett and was struck by his extraordinary story. David is an IANDS Board Member at Large. He is also the author of *Voyage of Purpose: Spiritual Wisdom from Near-Death Back to Life.*

David had such an awe-inspiring, near-death experience that I wanted to share it with you. It helps to illustrate the power of hope, prayer, and meditation. David's story is also a powerful example of the sort of life review that many people have, and the incredible, miraculous healing that is possible. What follows is David's story in his own words:

David Bennett: In my Near-Death Experience I had a life review, where I was shown parts of my future. Dealing with cancer was one of my future experiences. I was diagnosed with stage IV lung and bone cancer in November of 2000 with a very poor prognosis. It started in my lungs and metastasized into my spine where it ate two and a half of my thoracic bones causing my spine to collapse. They found lesions in my hip, kidney, and brain. I was told to get my affairs in order because I only had weeks to live.

Yet, because of my NDE and life experiences, acceptance of the cancer was immediate. It brought me back to my center and the balance of my human side and Spirit. It gave me new insights on how to deal with all aspects of coping with terminal illness. Cancer reminded me of how many lives we lovingly touch and work within our lives.

Gratefully, Spirit communicated many ways to deal with the physical pain, the drug induced highs and lows and the mental aspects of healing. I was shown practices of visualizations and meditations for relieving physical pain and to help in re-centering with the emotional anxieties and mood swings.

When cancer is initially diagnosed the very first fear that most people have is "Am I going to die?" This is the normal overwhelming first thought and most of the time there is no room for any other thought or emotion. The initial diagnosis will usually shock a person into some sort of action. The first action may be positive or negative and can be the beginning of the future path followed by that person.

The first few weeks the person will be in a fog and they may not even know it. Their thinking will be cloudy, and concentration might become difficult. It may be like they are zoning out. New contact with medical persons, however unwelcome, can tie up much of the mental and emotional energy you have.

I recommend making lists of questions for your meetings with medical personnel. Bring someone with you to those meetings because the fog will make it difficult for you to receive all the important information you are looking for. Remember, two heads are always better than one. Tell the other person what you are looking for and what you want.

With all this negative input and stimuli many people still experience a very positive and clearer insight on what is most important in their lives.

The process of letting go can open new doors to self-understanding. When someone begins their fight against a terminal illness, they struggle to keep that sense of control they are used to having. Total control during treatment is not possible.

Once a person gives up trying to control everything, they may start seeing aspects of themselves in their body, mind, and relationships in a new light. Their personal priorities may become clearer. Many survivors consider this heightened insight a positive result of their cancer experience.

Using Spiritual guidance, prayer, and visualization while combining traditional and holistic medicines, I was cancer free within six months.

David Bennett,

IANDS Board Member at Large, IANDS Local Groups Coordinator, and Author of *Voyage of Purpose: Spiritual Wisdom from Near-Death Back to Life.*

More Stories from Conquering Heroes

I hope you are as inspired by the above stories as I have been. It is truly astonishing what we can accomplish with God's help when we put our heart and mind into it.

When I first began reaching out to my friends and colleagues about sharing their own personal "conquering heroes" story, I was delighted with the warm and receptive response. I knew that each one of these individuals had a powerful story to share, and I believed that they would be open to sharing it if it would be of some benefit to others.

What I did not anticipate, however, was the remarkable excitement that this would generate, or how word of what we were doing would continue to spread. Nor did I imagine that this would lead to other people contacting me with their own "conquering heroes" story, or the story of someone they know. In fact, as we go to print, the stories keep coming in. If it continues at this rate, we will likely need to print a revised, expanded version of this book, or perhaps even another book altogether. Without a doubt, as with the stories above, as well as my own personal life history, many of the stories I'm reading are so remarkable that I feel compelled to get them into your hands as soon as I possibly can.

Consider, for example, the story of Sarah, a woman who was diagnosed with a serious type of Muscular Dystrophy (MD) when she was still in her early thirties. Sarah and her mother were so devastated by her diagnosis, that they proceeded to drive around the country, visiting with the leading MD experts, desperately hoping for a cure. When a number of top specialists told them that there was nothing that could be done, Sarah and her mother were understandably distraught.

With the rapid onset and progression of her disease, Sarah soon turned to a trusted life coach as a means of better dealing with what appeared to be a death sentence. When the life coach recommended that she start visualizing a more positive version of her life, Sarah thought the idea was a little strange. Nevertheless, she was willing to give it a try.

In time, Sarah really took to the practice, sometimes visualizing her ideal life in exquisite detail for several hours a day. She was really beginning to enjoy the experience too—far more than the reality of her life with Muscular Dystrophy.

But it wasn't until she started to imagine she was being healed that things really begin to change. Sarah eventually began a daily practice of visualizing herself being completely healed.

As a member of the LDS faith (the Church of Jesus Christ of Latter Day Saints), Sarah soon turned to the scriptures, searching for everything she could find related to Christ healing people in the Book of Mormon, and the New Testament. She would then visualize herself as the person Christ was healing, including the thoughts they had and the feelings they experienced before, during, and after they were healed. In her mind's eye, in vivid detail, she would see Christ's healing hands on her head, restoring her body and deteriorating muscles to their former strength. Sarah returned to specific passages again and again, including the words of Christ in the following passage from the Book of Mormon (3 Nephi 17:7-10):

""Have ye any that are sick among you? Bring them hither. Have ye any that are lame, or blind, or halt, or maimed, or leprous, or that are withered, or that are deaf, or that are afflicted in any manner? Bring them hither and I will heal them, for I have compassion upon you; my bowels are filled with mercy. For I perceive that ye desire that I should show unto you what I have done unto your brethren at Jerusalem, for I see that your faith is sufficient that I should heal you." And it came to pass that when he had thus spoken, all the multitude, with one accord, did go forth with their sick and their afflicted, and their lame, and with their blind, and with their dumb, and with all them that were afflicted in any manner; and he did heal them every one as they were brought forth unto him."

Suddenly, late one afternoon while lying alone on the beach outside her mother's home, visualizing herself being healed by Christ's hands on her head, something happened to Sarah. She felt as if her entire body had *actually, physically been healed*. Within days, Sarah slowly, but surely, began to see small, but noticeable improvements in her symptoms.

It has now been well over two decades, and Sarah is completely healed. Today, when she shares her miraculous story with others, Sarah will often quote from the Bible, Luke 4:40: "While the sun was setting, all those who had any who were sick with various diseases brought them to Him; and laying His hands on each one of them, He was healing them."

This incredible story about the extraordinary power of visualization is yet another one of the countless stories of people who have conquered any number of hopeless diseases, and, in the process, to the utter astonishment of the medical establishment, went on to live out the remainder of their God-given life on earth.

Will your story be next?

CHAPTER 54

A BOOK OF HOPE

Author's Concluding Note

Everyone has challenges. As my story and the stories above clearly illustrate, we all have our own unique trials and tribulations. This is a fact of life here on Earth. This life is a school, with custom-tailored problems. And though the problems we each face can be dramatically different, what is also clearly illustrated in the stories above and throughout this book is that the solutions to our problems have common themes.

Since the "Healing ALS Conference" in Salt Lake City, in 2019, I've had the opportunity to speak with many people who are in differing stages of ALS and their caregivers. I started a call-in prayer group meeting on Saturdays for anyone who feels the need for prayers and miracles.

One of the precious callers was a sweet woman named Rebecca, who was in a very advanced stage of ALS. She requested a copy of my book, *God's Heavenly Answers*, which I mailed to her.

After a few Saturdays with Rebecca on the prayer meeting call, I received a call from her mother, Sheila Hill, letting me know that Rebecca had passed to the Other Side. As we talked, we both felt a beautiful, sweet, and comforting feeling of peace, and knew it was Rebecca's time to go home to God.

Sheila continued to join us for the prayer meetings, and we had additional touching conversations privately. She also ordered several more books to send to family and friends with an inspiring note that they were being sent a gift from Rebecca.

Afterward, I received this special letter from Sheila as my gift from Rebecca, which I'm sharing with the world.

A Gift from Rebecca

With her Advanced stage of ALS, my daughter Rebecca, could no longer hold a book, so I read to her. How grateful I am that the last book we read together at the time of her passing was *God's*

Heavenly Answers by Dr. Joyce Brown. Rebecca also attended, by phone, Dr. Joyce's prayer meetings. (Anyone can attend— for more information go to HopeDr.org or call 877-375-6923.)

After Rebecca's passing what a comfort it was for me to attend the prayer meeting and to talk with Dr. Joyce about my beloved Rebecca. Because of Dr. Joyce's near-death experience, she has knowledge of the Other Side.

Some of the topics of her book are: *Take time to listen to the whisperings of the Spirit, Caring relationships do not end at death, Mingling with angels, Words can hurt, We learn from each other, Each of us has a purpose, True empowerment comes from God, Forgiveness brings glorious freedom, Time is too limited to hold grudges, and The truth and beauty of the Scriptures.*

I feel that this book and prayer meeting were a gift from Rebecca.

Sheila Hill, January 11, 2021

It's so important that we understand that this world is not the real world. The Other Side is real. And eternal. The key, therefore, to solving the problems we have begins with having an eternal perspective.

God is real. Courage and faith matter. Prayer works. When you pray to God, you are opening yourself up to a world of limitless possibilities. When you pray, you are putting yourself in the way of miracles.

It's important to forgive yourself and others. It's important to have faith. Believe in miracles, expect miracles, and *be* a miracle for someone else. This last part is just as important as the second and the first. Help those around you however you can. When you help others, you help yourself. Even small actions may lead to great benefits.

The popular motivational speaker, Barry Shore—who also has a remarkable story of recovering from a crippling disease, one which left him completely paralyzed—says that "HOPE means: Helping Other People Everyday," and SMILE means "See Miracles in Life Everyday." Whenever you are wondering HOW in your life, Barry often tells his audiences, remember the answer is "Help Others Win."

As it was revealed to me during my near-death experience, the Scriptures are true. The wisdom of a number of them specifically stood out to me. The first one is: "If ye love me, keep my commandments."[John 14:15, (All Scriptures are KJV)]

The two greatest commandments are:

"Thou shalt love the Lord thy God with all thy heart, and with all thy soul, and with all thy mind."[Matthew 22:37]

"And the second is like unto it, Thou shalt love thy neighbour as thyself."[Matthew 22:39]

As we give, so shall we receive.

Also, what was shown to me was the truth and importance of the Sermon on the Mount. Here are some highlights that stood out.

"Blessed are they that mourn: for they shall be comforted."[Matthew 5:4]

"Blessed are they which do hunger and thirst after righteousness: for they shall be filled."[Matthew 5:6]

"Blessed are the merciful: for they shall obtain mercy."[Matthew 5:7]

"Blessed are the pure in heart: for they shall see God."[Matthew 5:8]

"Blessed are the peacemakers: for they shall be called the children of God."[Matthew 5:9]

"Let your light so shine before men, that they may see your good works, and glorify your Father which is in heaven."[Matthew 5:6]

". . . Pray for them which despitefully use you and persecute you."[Matthew 5:44]

"Judge not, that ye be not judged."[Matthew 7:1]

Let the light of hope and joy shine in your eyes as you look out at the world and those around you.

Take time to stop and breathe deeply. Have good thoughts about yourself and others.

One of the best ways to reduce stress, depression, and grief is by using our Earth time wisely, and lovingly helping others. Time and how we use it is vitally important. Maintaining an eternal perspective of your time can help you attain peace of mind, and can help ensure you enjoy the Other Side when you get there. I think the following proverb is great advice:

> *"Yesterday is but a dream*
>
> *And tomorrow is only a vision*
>
> *But today well lived [making good use of time]*
>
> *Makes every yesterday a dream of happiness*
>
> *And every tomorrow a vision of hope."*

It's almost like magic the miracles we can make happen when we embrace eternal perspectives with faith, prayer and persistence. Miracles often come after you've done all you can, and there is no other way.

As I hope this book and the stories above have made abundantly clear, regardless of the problem you are facing, giving up is not a successful option. Problems are opportunities to learn and grow. Challenges are stepping-stones to drawing on the powers of Heaven. Every adversity you face carries hidden benefits within. You just have to keep on keeping on until you discover what those benefits are.

The following poem I have been reading and sharing every year since I wrote it in 1960:

> *"Coming soon is a bright new year*
>
> *As it comes closer and ever near*
>
> *I know within me, without a doubt*
>
> *Its joys are so many, I could almost shout.*
>
> *First on the list is guidance and love,*
>
> *Given from our Heavenly Father above.*
>
> *Also there will be a bright new day*
>
> *Given to teach in its own special way*

Also wisdom and knowledge are sure to be there

If only I try and show that I care.

This next New Year can't help but be fine

Because all of these gifts are already mine."

—Joyce Hunt Brown "A Bright New Year" (1960)

EMPOWERING BONUS SUPPLEMENTS

APPENDIX

Words of Wisdom

I have had many miracles in my life, and you can too. A key part of creating miracles is adopting the right attitude. Read and reread the following few pages, and watch as your mind is renewed.

I share these with you from my heart to yours, with love and prayers for special blessings,

—Dr. Joyce Hunt Brown

Enjoy Life, This is Not a Dress Rehearsal

Look for, find, and create happiness.

Life is like a game. But the real score is mostly kept on the Other Side.

Giving up doesn't work. Earth time is limited.

It is worth finding out how to make certain you enjoy the Other Side when you get there.

As we give, so shall we receive.

Life demands that we confront situations. Sometimes we have to change the situation. Other times we need to change ourselves.

Prayer, wisdom, and God's inspiration will help us to know the difference.

Enjoy life. This is not a dress rehearsal.

Have an Awesome Day

The first law of learning is repetition. Read this with sincere enthusiasm and heartfelt intent every morning when you first wake up, and every night just before you go to sleep. This will do wonders in helping you to create miraculous results. If you want to have better thinking, feelings and actions, read this every morning and evening.

For Now…I will be cheerful, loving and kind

For Now…I will try to adjust myself to what "is;"

Not try to adjust everything to my own desires.

For Now…I will speak softly, be calm, patient and forgiving.

For Now…I will do a good turn or a kind deed.

For Now…I will be as agreeable as I can.

For Now…I will try to live through this day only.

For Now…I will give myself at least a half hour for meditating, counting my blessings, and giving thanks for what I have.

For Now…I will have faith, be confident, and express gratitude.

For Now…I will look for the good in everyone and everything.

For Now…I will remember to breathe deeply and smile often.

Every adversity carries with it seeds of benefits—the challenge is to "keep on keeping on" until we find the benefits.

Look for, find, and create joy and happiness for yourself and others.

Desire, visualize, and realize.

—Dr. Joyce Hunt Brown

The Power of Words

Words have tremendous power. They can build or destroy relationships. They can determine the direction of your life.

Like arrows, once a word is spoken it cannot be called back. One of life's greatest challenges is to harness the tongue!

Words can hit like a fist and hurt, or they can soothe, comfort, guide and teach. How we use words to hurt or help others is our choice—their reaction is not. Words are powerful tools for influencing others and can pace, lead, and direct our thoughts. They can even influence the direction of our destiny.

Words lead our thinking and form mental pictures. As an example, what would come to your mind if I told you NOT to think about a pink elephant? You just thought of a pink elephant, didn't you? In fact, the more I would tell you not to think about the big pink elephant with yellow ears and big green spots, the more vivid the picture of her would come into your mind. Even if you forced yourself to think of something else, you had to think about the big pink elephant first in order to know what it was you were not supposed to think about.

Our words create attitudes and mental pictures for others. Our attitudes toward other people, and our thoughts create our mental pictures which greatly influences the words we speak to others. We can attract others to us or push them away by our words. Therefore, it is important to choose our words carefully. Words can have a strong positive or negative effect—all by themselves.

Words to Avoid (for Better Relationships)

A book of rules includes the following list of words to make a point. However, when they are used in conversations, the words are usually perceived as being harsh. In fact, they may automatically set a negative polarity in the other person and tend to take away the person's own power and free-will. Some of these words act as commands; others diminish any exceptions to a differing opinion. Often, these words can make the other person feel "cornered" and they may be detrimental to a

195

relationship.

- **SHOULD**
- **OUGHT**
- **MUST**
- **HAVE TO**
- **ALL**
- **EVERY**
- **ALWAYS**
- **NEVER**
- **TRY**
- **BUT**
- **CAN'T**
- **DON'T**
- **IMPOSSIBLE**

Replacement Words

The following words and word combinations are "fluffy words." They expand parameters. They tend to empower the other person and encourage them to search for options. They are also good words to improve relationships. These words are very useful in teaching as they lead people into thinking and becoming more self-disciplined.

- **IF**
- **WHAT IF**
- **HOW**
- **HOW WOULD YOU FEEL**
- **MAY**
- **YOU MAY WANT TO**
- **PERHAPS YOU COULD**
- **PERHAPS**
- **CURIOUS**
- **WONDER**
- **SO**
- **AND**

"If I understand you correctly…"

This is one of the most effective phrases to encourage others to think and talk!

Six Important Words:

"I am sorry." and "I love you."

More important than what we say is what someone *perceives* we said.

We are all still learning, and we are all at our own level of growth. Others react and learn from our words. Our words and their tone can help create more harmony in our life, in our home, and in our relationships. We can reap heavenly and miraculous results with our words. And as the Scriptures teach us,

"Whatsoever we soweth, that also shall we reap."

Touching the Future

My three children, Suzan, Patty, and David are all grown and have children and grand-children of their own. I now have 13 grandchildren, 30 great-grandchildren, and 2 great-great-grandchildren, so there are currently 5 generations for a total of 48 direct descendants at the present time. To me, they're all gifted and special and I love them all.

Even though we love and care for each other, we don't get to see each other in person as often as we would like. We try to keep in contact, sharing life's major events.

Five generations. Dr. Joyce (top right) with her grandmother, mother, daughter and baby granddaughter.

I was very touched and surprised to receive these heart-warming letters. They reminded me once again just how much our words matter, and how the impact we have on one another can last a lifetime and, in some cases, even echo across generations.

From my great-granddaughter, Brooklynn, at age 11.

Dear Grandma Joyce,

Thank you for everything. You are so wonderfully nice and outstanding. You're above and beyond amazing. You are also fantastic. I'm very glad to be your great-granddaughter. You're very sweet and terrific. And I'm being honest. I love you very, very much. Love,

Brooklynn

Wouldn't any grandmother love to receive a letter like this? I loved it so much that I framed it, and, now more than three years later, it still hangs on my wall.

A Selection of Precious Memories with Treasured Stories

Precious Memories with Treasured Stories

Precious Memories with Treasured Stories

Precious Memories with Treasured Stories

Precious Memories with Treasured Stories

Precious Memories with Treasured Stories

Precious Memories with Treasured Stories

Precious Memories with Treasured Stories

Precious Memories with Treasured Stories

Precious Memories with Treasured Stories

Precious Memories with Treasured Stories

Precious Memories with Treasured Stories

Precious Memories with Treasured Stories

ABOUT THE AUTHOR

Joyce Hunt Brown, Ph.D., N.D., E.F.T., Author, Speaker, and Coach, Founder and President of Stress and Grief Relief, Inc.

Dr. Joyce Brown, after having multiple symptoms and health problems for some time, was finally diagnosed with ALS in May of 1988, at the age of 54. She had severe difficulties with weak muscles and choking on her own saliva. She had breathing problems which required oxygen. Along with having to wear a neck and ankle brace, constant twitching and atrophy of her muscles, she had a hard time walking or holding her head up. Communicating became more and more difficult as she lost most of her voice.

She went to a top M.D. who specialized in homeopathy and acupuncture. He diagnosed her with ALS and Myasthenia Gravis (MG). Though in shock and disbelief, she decided to start homeopathic treatments immediately. Not believing she had ALS, she consulted another doctor who gave her the same diagnoses. Still in denial, she consulted a neurologist familiar with ALS. His testing and diagnosis was: ALS with 5 months to live!

She continued her treatments which also included heart-felt prayers, dietary changes, along with meditating and listening to unique *sleep learning* with positive affirmations from her own recordings *Whispers for Life and Prosperity* and *Whispers for Miraculous Results*.

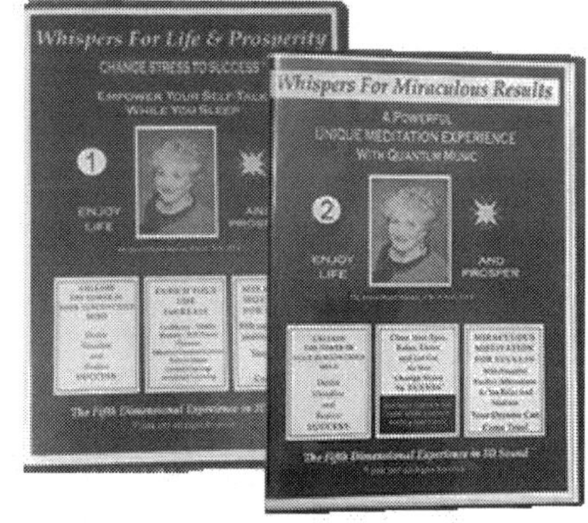

Amazingly, with God's power, after beginning the

homeopathic remedies that Dr. Khoe ordered from Germany, she was healed of ALS and had no after-effects, even completely recovering her voice.

Moving forward with new energy and resilience, she became a licensed Naturopathic Doctor. She continues to work with world renowned scientists, quantum physicists, medical doctors, and health specialists.

While in practice as an N.D., Dr. Joyce was credited with improving and saving many lives. She has received six Lifetime Achievement Awards in the natural health field. Even though she is in a power chair because of an auto accident in 2003 which left her with continuous, extreme pain, and the loss of much of her vision in 2014, she remains very active. Now almost 90 years of age, with a vibrant voice, she is a professional speaker, coach, counselor and President of the non-denominational, non-profit organization, Stress and Grief Relief, Inc.

She helps people change stress to success and find their true purpose for living, with unique coping techniques for depression, anger management, and suicide prevention. She has authored many books, including the best seller, *God's Heavenly Answers: Near Death Experience Revealed*; and her most recent book, *Near Death Survivor Conquers ALS, Blindness, Depression, Grief, Suicide and More, a Book of Hope: I've Had Many Miracles and YOU Can Too*. Her forthcoming books include, *What to Do Before and After the Doctor Says, "Nothing More Can Be Done." and The Secret Life of a Little Service Dog Named Kitty, and Proof She Went to Heaven.*

Dr. Joyce works tirelessly as a Chaplain, sharing God's message of hope, reasons for living and the wondrous reality that there is life after life! She continues helping others with crisis management, including troubled teens, inmates, and all others needing her special skills. She is known today as "The Therapist's Therapist," and, on television, as "The Hope Doctor," but her favorite title is HRE, "Heavenly Retirement

Expert." She understands the true value of our limited Earth time and wants to share the knowledge obtained in her Near-Death Experience of 1983.

Her websites are:

www.HopeDr.org and www.StressAndGriefRelief.org

As time permits, Dr. Joyce accepts speaking requests. If you would like to be notified when she may be in an area near you, please write to her or send an email with your name, location, and contact information.

GET IN TOUCH TODAY

Do you have questions? Do you need a book, or know someone who really needs a book? Do you have a story to tell about how this book helped you or a loved one? Please contact Dr. Joyce by mail, email, or phone:

Stress and Grief Relief, Inc.
450 Hillside Dr., Suite A224
Mesquite, NV, 89027
1-800-734-3439
www.HopeDr.org
www.StressAndGriefRelief.org

AskDrJoyce@yahoo.com

All profits from this book are donated to helping others. Would you like to help us make this book available to organizations, churches, prisons, and groups, including troubled youth? Stress and Grief Relief, Inc., 501(c)(3), is a life-changing and lifesaving non-profit organization. All donations are tax deductible.

Help Us Save Lives!

We have a big message, and we need your help! Suicide is not the answer. Please join with us, and become a lifesaver by helping us share Dr. Joyce's story. If you can, please make a donation today so we can reach more people with The Hope Doctor's message of hope: "Life is worth living, and loving, even with all of its challenges!"

ACKNOWLEDGMENTS

First and foremost, I want to thank **God** with heartfelt gratitude for all the miracles I've had in my life, for being able to write this book, and for all of the following people who have been a part of God's plan to get this message out to the world.

With tremendous appreciation, I want to acknowledge all those who have helped this book become a reality. I especially want to thank **Patricia Tamowski, Scott Douglas**, and **Lisa Feiner** who started me on this journey. This began as a chapter about my miraculous, complete healing of ALS in 1988. The chapter is part of their upcoming book about ALS reversals. Lisa Feiner is co-founder of SharpAgain.org, an organization committed to a world where dementia can be prevented, treated and even reversed. Patricia and Scott are co-founders of HealingALS.org. They encouraged me to write a full-length book about my miracle-filled life. They also interviewed me about my story, including my near-death experience and miraculous healing of ALS (which is available on YouTube as "Dr. Joyce Brown's ALS Reversal Story Part 1" and "Dr. Joyce Brown Q&A Part 2"). You can learn the latest information about ALS on their website at HealingALS.org

I want to thank my good friend **Tina Foster**, whom I've known for many years. Along with being a professional writer and editor, Tina is an author with several published books. Tina helped me get the words down while I dictated over the phone. My low vision makes it virtually impossible to type on a computer. But Tina was willing to spend many hours on the phone with me each day, sending different versions back and forth by email to review and edit. It was very tedious working over the phone, which went on for nearly twelve months. Bless her heart, that she stuck with me to the end of the book. I love her a lot.

My dear friend **Dr. David W. Allan**, an atomic clock scientist, and author of *It's About Time: Science Harmonizing with Religion,* has been a great encourager to me. Dr. Allan is a world-renowned atomic clock physicist who helped develop the nation's atomic clock during his 32 years at NBS/NIST (National Institute of Standards and Technology). He spent many years helping in the development of GPS. During that time, he created the smallest measurement of time, known as *Allan's Variance,* which was needed to develop GPS and more. He lectures to top scientists all over the world and has received the highest scientific awards. He and his wife Edna have been my best friends since 2001 when they read my book *God's Heavenly Answers.* Their prayers and encouragement have been a vital part of my life, including getting this book written and published.

Jan Stivers Wilkinson is retired from the editorial team of the *Better Homes and Gardens* magazine. She also ran three remarkably successful businesses. Jan is exceptionally experienced in the business world, and her willingness to share her vast knowledge and skills has been a gift from God. She has helped me in getting this book out, and a number of other critical responsibilities. I am thankful for her help with our non-profit as well.

I greatly appreciate the board members of **Stress and Grief Relief, Inc.,** especially their encouragement and support, and their collective dedication to our cause—it has been priceless. We could not have done all that we have done without their support, including: **June Davidson**, Ph.D., an international life coach, and the President of American Seminar Leaders Association. June is just a remarkable woman who has long been an inspiration to me

personally. **David Hodgson, Esq.**, I so appreciate his guidance and dedication to our mission to change and save lives. **Romaine Tuft**, RN, a woman both wonderful and wise who

will forever have my gratitude and admiration. There are not enough words to express my love and appreciation for Romaine, who always seems to be there when I really need her. We always have so much fun when we're together. I want to mention **Patricia Tamowski** again for her invaluable contribution to our board, and for her and her husband Scott Douglas' world-saving dedication to helping all those with ALS. And, of course, **Jim Quick**, who has graciously guided us through the intricate legal requirements of our non-profit organization. Thanks to all of you for your encouragement in getting this book out.

An additional Earth Angel is **Jon Welsh,** who has been a valuable instrument in God's hands in helping this project become a reality. He designed the cover, and did all of the layout and formatting work, along with much of the editing, to get the manuscript ready to be printed and published. Along with working as the director of our content marketing, he is a dedicated life-saver for me, this book, and all those who will read and benefit from it.

I would like to acknowledge **Bill Sardi,** who has been a special blessing in my life. I believe Bill has a direct line to Heaven. He is also the author of twelve books on health, many  of which offer information not available anywhere else. I greatly appreciate the work he does, his encouragement and support, and his miraculous vision-saving supplement Longevinex. We have been able to save and change many lives as a result of Bill's generosity in making books available for our non-profit, Stress and Grief Relief, Inc.

I would like to thank my priceless friend and colleague **Dr. Calzada** for his continuous encouragement, wisdom, and support.

I also want to acknowledge those outstanding people who have shared their stories, and who have all lived interesting and heroic lives, including:

- **Judi Moreo,** international speaker, author, and life coach, who has added invaluable input on this book. Judi is an exceptionally good friend, we have become like sisters. My day is always brighter when we get a chance to talk.

- Author, speaker and co-founder of Yokel Local **Stormie Andrews,** who has opened doors of opportunity that we otherwise would not have.

- Internationally recognized hall of fame speaker **Dan Clark,** who shares my deep, heartfelt commitment to helping others.

- Best-selling author and top Hollywood story consultant, **Michael Hauge** whose personal example captured my attention, and who inspired me to think more deeply about the importance of storytelling, and how we use stories to connect with each other.

- Keynote speaker, author, consultant, and master herbalist

Clive Buchanan. Along with being a special friend, Clive is an absolute powerhouse on the platform. His audiences are captivated from the moment he first begins.

- I want to thank **Aimmee Kodachian** for sharing her remarkable story of transformation. Aimmee is a bright light of sunshine in the world, and we have become special friends with the shared goal of giving hope to the hopeless.

- **Dr. Vern Kilbourn** and his wife, **Barbara**, who have become great friends and encouragers in getting this book finished.

- Author, speaker, and consultant **Anthony DeNino**, who has been a big help in getting this book's message out to the world.

- **Dr. William Moulton** and his wife, **Janeen**, who have been very dear friends and encouragers to me and the work of our non-profit.

- **David Bennett,** author of *Voyage of Purpose: Spiritual Wisdom from Near-Death Back to Life.* His story is one that has and will continue to help many people.

- **Dr. Wendell Robertson**, DDS, a world-renowned holistic dentist, and a true friend and a great encourager of getting this book out.

- **Dr. Jack Hinkle**, D.O., an osteopathic physician, a true life-line, and a great supporter to help get this book out to the world, and our message to prevent suicide.

I want to thank my precious granddaughter **Krystal Conklin** for being so giving of her time, and for her tremendously valuable input. She has been there for me at some of the most critical times in my life.

I want to thank **John Chau, D.D.S.** for his priceless support and encouragement in helping to save lives. Dr. Chau and I have shared some Heavenly experiences together, and I greatly appreciate his willingness to help us fulfill our mission.

I also want to acknowledge **Melisa Wells-Murphy**, who has become a good friend as well as a reliable source for some of the latest top scientific health classes and information.

I would also like to give a special thanks to **Jose and Hilda Cruz** who are like family and have done so many things to help me, including helping me get

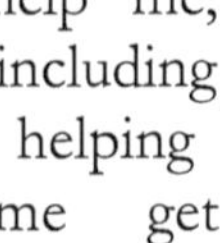

this book out. They are eager to see this book translated into Spanish.

A special thanks to my good friend **Louise White Pledge**, who is a wonderful communicator and an absolute master grammarian.

Other Earth Angels and contributors to this book include my special, wonderfully talented great-granddaughter **Jaiden,** as well as my dear friends **Cathy Carroll, Carol Thatcher, Nancy Jackson, Bob and Donna Rudy, Billy Triplet, Mary Kae Washburn, Joan Day, Tana Parr, Jody Krouth,** and **Sheila Hill.**

A special thanks to those who participate in our weekly Reap a Miracle World-Wide Prayer Group for their encouragement for getting this book out. I especially want to express my sincere thanks and appreciation to my daughters, **Suzan Stalford,** and **Patty Taylor,** for their time and dedication in making sure each week we hear their meaningful, and empowering contributions. Participants have told me that Suzan's and Patty's heartfelt presentations of "How to Have an Awesome Day" have truly helped in such a way that they really feel it within and that it helps brighten their day.

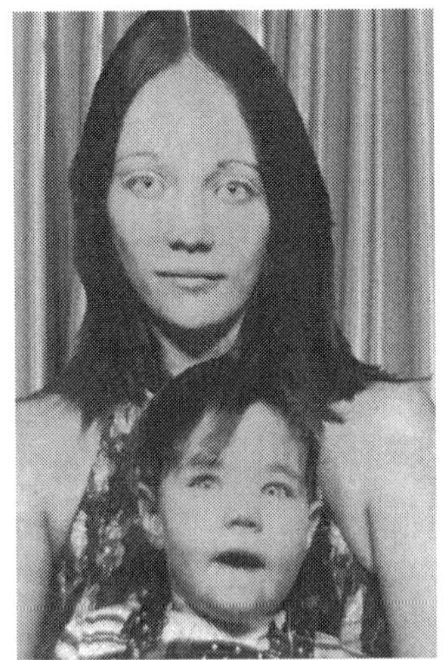

Finally, I want to recognize and thank those people who are going to help get this book distributed to those who are in need of its messages throughout the world, as well as all the people who have motivated me to get this book out. And to all those people who have ALS and are struggling to reverse it, including their care givers, and families, may God guide and bless you throughout your lives.

Want to Enrich and Improve Your Life with a Powerful, Proven Sleep Learning System?

"Dr. Joyce Brown's Sleep Learning System is a great gift
to humanity. It will truly 'Change Stress to Success.'"
—Richard Bennett, R.N.

Recent university research yet again confirms what Dr. Joyce has been teaching for decades: You *can* learn while you sleep. You can unleash the power of your unconscious mind while you sleep and reap incredible, lasting changes in your life as a result. With powerful, positive affirmations, you can change your self-talk and transform your life. With this breakthrough system, your dreams *can* come true. Get this powerful, scientifically-proven *sleep learning* system today and you will Unleash the power of your unconscious mind to:

- Increase your Self-Confidence
- Boost your Energy and Vitality
- Relieve Stress and Reduce Anxiety
- Improve your Willpower and Self-Control
- Strengthen your Relationships
- Change Stress to Success

"I have personally used Dr. Joyce Hunt Brown's sleep learning recordings and find them positive, uplifting, and inspiring. Every affirmation for SUCCESS has been included, and every one is positive."
—Dr. Ralph Ellsworth

For more information about this sleep learning system, plus other unique coping techniques, how it can benefit you, and your family, and friends, visit: www.HopeDoctor.org/shop or call: toll free: (800) 675-1777

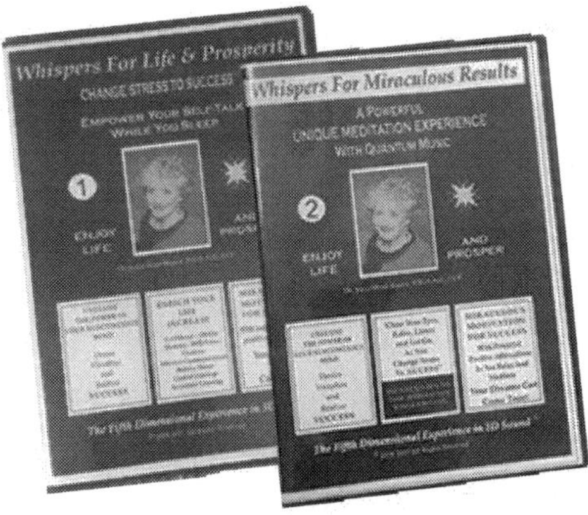

Made in the USA
Columbia, SC
07 October 2021

46450297R00128